Donna Kessler

Swirling Emotions

Poetic Therapy

Dedicated to the memory of my father,
Peter Kessler, who has passed.
Rest in peace.

Contents

Her Gravitational Pull

She rests in the sky, the silver lines on her orange shaped
body twinkle in the night. She swims in the sea, pulling
at the tides then pushing them away. I sink into the flow
of her hands while she moves me into a peaceful dream.

She shines in the night while gentle clouds pass
by her, bowing down to her elegance and her
radiating presence. She cradles me in her arms while
I sink into a restful slumber, her warmth like fresh,
silky sheets. I gravitate towards her illuminating
aura. She is a poised phantom in the night.

She rises with the stars then sinks into the daylight.
She hides in the shadows of the sun, waiting until
her time comes to reappear so she can shine a
glamorous glow onto the land beneath her. Beasts
howl in the night, honoring her sharp presence.

I sing a melodic tune into the night, my face pressed
against the window. I stare up at her beauty. I wish I
could fly to her and sit among the stars by her side, high
above the world, serenity engulfing me like a fire.

A Long Time Gone

The plane descends upon the desert landscape.
I watch in awe as large, cactus-filled mountains
reach my view. My eyes gaze upon the unknown
area. I shift and squirm in the prickly seat. I wonder
what will happen from my sudden appearance.

The door I had locked to keep out the people
whose blood ran through mine crumbled to ash.
The rocky barrier no longer stood between us.

I walk into the house which contains no memories of
my presence. I see photos on the walls of a different life
and a bitter sensation claws its way to the edge of my
skin. The hairs on my arm prickle and my hands clench,
then unclench. There are shadows of the past which
follow me throughout the wooden house, reminding me
of the water that lies heavily underneath the bridge.

Tension hangs in the air. You await my excuse
for being a long time gone. I shrug and bite my
tongue, resisting the itch to release my claws.

I discover remnants of my younger self and I sneer at
her. I turn my back and set the pictures down which
contain only ghosts and memories which I do not recall.

I wander through the halls. There is so much change, but I merely blame myself for being gone for so long. I am the villain who has been hiding in my cave, snarling at anybody who dared to come close to the entrance.

Old resentments melt. The guilt gnaws at me like a predator, chewing at me like a delicious bone.

I have been gone a long time. Everything has changed. The people who I grew up with are suddenly unknown as the realization dawns on me that they are black cats in the dark. Their souls are hidden behind locked doors which I pound on but cannot open. There is a murky shadow hanging above me whispering words of madness and deceit.

I lie in the heavy comforter at night in the room where frames are hung on the wall of the life which I refused to live in; they are a taunting presence. There is a tornado of doubt tossing me around like a limp, torn doll.

Daylight comes and shines down onto me, the pellucid sun breathing an aroma of roses into my senses. My heart defrosts from the frozen state. There is a merry bounce in my step as I greet the relatives who I have shut out as I left them in the dust. Perhaps it is time I return home to the safe, comforting arms of love. Gratitude fills the void within me, the darkness concealed within a box.

Forgiveness makes a nest inside my heart made of tar.

"Welcome home," they tell me. I smile. I walk into
the light and breathe in the smell of homemade
pancakes and fruit. I dive into the relishing sensation
of coming home. The pain slithers out of my skin
and the tender wings of affection embrace me.

Grateful

Gratitude hovers above me
tapping my shoulder
when darkness sweeps over
as I lie down to sleep.

"You have so much to be thankful for."

Soothing words
floating from the lips of angels
brightening the day.

I smile,
my eyes drift shut.

I count my blessings like sheep
clutching them like a blanket
so, they do not float away.

Discovery of Intimacy

Blue lingerie and bare skin, there was tenderness in the depth of your eyes. You spoke erotic words to me, complimenting my alluring presence. You slipped the fabric down my shoulders. You smiled adoringly, your eyes shining like a ray of light. You inhaled my jasmine scented perfume, breathing it in like it was your oxygen.

We fell onto the bed in a passionate entanglement, our limbs connecting, our hearts beating as one. There was an innocent gentleness in the way we touched. You held me in your arms like a fragile glass. Your eyes melted into goo as you stared at my beauty, taking it in as if I were a glamorous, vibrant painting. You touched my hands softly and caressed my smooth, pale skin. Your hands wandered over my curvy body, grazing my skin, sending shivers down my spine and tingles between my thighs.

Your skin was warm and enveloped me like a cozy fleece blanket. Your hair was soft and thick as I ran my hands through it and your rough lips suckled on my skin. Your head lay in the curve of my neck as you buried yourself into me, breathing melodic sighs of happiness into my ears.

Butterflies and fireworks erupted within me; passionate red colors exploded between us. I wrapped myself into you. Your adoration for me consumed my soul. I felt myself fall deeper into a hypnotizing trance filled with love for you.

You turned me into a blossoming rose. You plucked out the thorns and covered me with petals, showering me with seeds of endearment.

The discovery of intimacy is sacred and blissful. You kept me safe in your strong arms. You brought me close to you and never let me go. You cradled my head and loved me whole. You kept my secrets and accepted the ugly, embracing the good. Your tantalizing blarney pulled me into your enticing starry soul.

The discovery of intimacy is pure,
discovering it with you was divine.

The Bliss You Gave Me

Your cotton hands caress my satin flesh. Your body
encases me in a warm cocoon. Warm drizzles of bliss
travel throughout my body, sending tingles to my toes.

You coat me with red and pink tulips.

Your eyes resemble the beaming sun. Our blissful
ardor carries me into moonlit stars, my soul absorbed
by the magic of the Alaskan aurora borealis.

You spill your blood upon my exposed flesh, slashing
me with your sword of passion. You appear in
my oracular dreams, casting a spell onto me.

Everything is connected. We bloom, we
soar, we sink into heavenly clouds.

Living on My Own

Loneliness creeps upon me, keeping me company
in the dark era of my life. I scavenge and shove stale
scraps of food down my throat like a wild animal.
Money is heaped into a pile of logs and burnt in ash.

I blindly run in circles, my body collapsing into walls and
shattering like glass. My mentality is fragile, gripping onto
anything that keeps me from sinking into black pits of hell.

Uncertainty claws at my skin and my thoughts go
round and round like a nauseating Ferris Wheel. Did I
make the right decision? Why must living be so hard?

I am a mere seventeen-year-old girl. My childhood is
ripped out from under me like a rug. There are stones
placed upon my back. Inky shadows dance upon the walls
in the darkness of the night. The rooms remain empty.

Vermin made of bones and decaying flesh
prowl in the shadows, gliding nails along the
sandpaper wall, screeching and moaning.

Skeleton hands reach for my throat in the
nightfall, invading my slumber.
A haunted ashen face floats in my
vision, stopping my heart.

I sit in solitude; days go by and time becomes mingled. My home resides within a kingdom of shadows. My dreams consist of loss and failure.

Where did everybody go? Resentment fills me to the core, and I shut out my family. I lock the door, refusing to glance at who is knocking to be let in. Rotten thoughts engulf my mind, burning me from the inside out. They are wretched, filthy rats, they become squashed beneath my unforgiving feet.

I am lurching across a crimson bridge. I am banished into the raven black darkness away from the celestial light, living as a beldam. My soul is plagued to wander woefully, suffering within brick walls of squalor. I am hypnotized within a hole of bone breaking tumult.

Blind fury damages my eyesight. The waves are immense. They bury me. The ghostly echoes of the past ring in my ear.

My feet slip. I fall into the bottom of a rocky slope; the sharp edges of stones cut me open, bloody guts spilling out. My limbs break. Nauseating flashbacks tear at my head. I open my eyes and repair myself like a newborn doll. I stand up and brush off the dirt, determination to start over evident on my worn-down face.

Eighteen years old comes upon me and suddenly I
am thrown into a new beginning. I transform from
a small, helpless bug into a confident butterfly.
The impending lonesomeness simmers into a small
flame. I toss the demons that come out to play. My
apartment becomes brighter; my cry for hunger
diminishes as food is piled into my fridge.

Adulthood knocks on my door and I let it in
cautiously. I grow from my regrettable mistakes.

My mailbox is filled with bills, money
flows in then flows out.

A radiance is placed onto my dull lips. My
thinning hair grows back into a thick mane.
I walk among the living, resembling a newly
grown flower, glowing like a ray of sunshine

I fall into a delusion of living in a perfect fantasy. The walls
eventually come crumbling down, revealing the damage.

My arms thrash. I am pulled underneath the unforgiving
whitecaps. Black crows whisper in the darkness, my
demons await, grasping my throat when the moon rises.

A deep sense of panic takes control, tossing me into
a whirling tornado. My disastrous emotions are
swarming like bees above me, stinging my flesh.

The truth rushes into me at full force. I am my own enemy. I cannot live if I am living in the past. I cannot be better if I am frozen.

Dawn rises. A golden song hovers above rich green meadow. Rusted hinges creak with age. The sun breaths freedom onto my face. My heart soars. I gambol away from tenebrous walls which suffocate my lungs. Spellbinding felicity consumes me.

Nineteen years old comes around the corner. I have been on my own for over two years. I accept the new coming of age era. I shake my head disappointingly while I think back to the young, helpless, traumatized girl who first began living on her own. I embrace her and tell her that everything turned out alright. She can fly away now.

I nourish my body and tend to my mental needs. The fog has lifted from my vision and suddenly everything is clear. I no longer pick at old festering wounds. The pain is stitched, healing with time.

Living on my own saved me from a hanging disaster that had been waiting to pour down onto me. Living on my own dragged me away from the baggage and lifted me out of the river filled with mud.

Living on my own dug everything out of me and tore
out my raw emotions, dissecting me piece by piece.
Living on my own taught me the secrets of surviving
and pushed me to become a better version of myself.
It was all I needed to pull myself out of the abyss in
order to thrive in this chaotic world. I am now twenty.
Everything has fallen into place. I have found serenity.

Sway

I wish to sway with you
in the wind.

We soar
through the sky.

We sail
through the blue
of the sea.

Eternity

Dewy drops of mist upon the early morning grass.
Rays of sunlight seep through the glass windows.

Birds sit upon the windowsill,
singing melodic tunes.

Mornings with you are serene rippling lakes.
Mornings with you send tingles through my silky skin.
You caress my hand, intertwining us together.

Strawberry kisses,
pancakes and sweet crumbling muffins,
our sparkling hearts connecting.

I send prayers to the heavens above
wishing upon a star
for our red, soft love
to be a never-ending story.

We sink into a thundering passion.
We grow together like wildflowers.
We are a deer and doe prancing
in a dancing meadow.

Darkness to Light

I stumble through the dark, sobbing while my limbs break. I fall into a haze of unnerving madness. The world around me spins in a blur, my stomach grumbles with anger. A shadow of solitude following my footsteps, I become lost in the overcast nightfall.

A voice speaks within the worn-down walls of my body. The susurrus of the Atlantic waves calls me to sink beneath the dark mist of the egregious trenches. The diaphanous reflection of the paradisiacal sky fades from my blurry vision.

A ladder appears. I climb up the sticks, soaring above the water and into the light. Demons have followed me through my life; heartbreak has tumbled my way; bruises have formed on top of my skin. The darkness sweeps over horrifically, covering my world with blackness. The cycle of terror ends, the pain is healed, and the wounds begin to close. The infection is cured.

A rainbow rises in the horizon; the sky becomes baby blue and birds chirp in the mornings. Lessons have been taught; my legs have strengthened, and I leap over obstacles with grace. My arms, which were once weak, now carry the weight of the rocks. I drop the rocks into the dirt and bury them with a shovel.

Darkness will come, but then it will pass. It will transform into a bright beam of light. The flowers will bloom once more; the barren land will grow during the arrival of summer.

My lips turn into a smile. The gloomy darkness becomes a glowing light. My troubles fade into the dust. Little seeds of change and prosperity are planted. A new beginning grows from the ground.

The universe hears my cries; it pats my back and grants me my wishes. I thrive.

Lola

My sweet Lola, her coat is sleek, her ears are pointed
elegantly. Her snout to the ground as she sniffed and
scoured through the dirt. Her black and tan markings
gleamed in the night. Her bark protective as she guarded
the log cabin and its inhabitants. My hands which patted
her back and held her paws, my eyes shone with joy as my
unpredictable father walked in with a newborn Doberman.

Oh Lola, you were my light, you were my happiness. Your
smooth tongue licked my soft child-like face. My sweet
Lola, you ran freely through the open yard. Your spirit
had been as bright as a yellow dandelion, you trotted
through the paddocks and playfully chased the goats.

Oh Lola, you would not hurt a soul. Why
would such a terrible act happen to you?

Panic rose in my throat and goosebumps covered
my skin as I searched day through night for
you, your disappearance cut me and tore me
to pieces. Oh Lola, where did you go?

A deathly rotten scent wafted through the air. A
trail of blood stained the grass, your mangled body
lay on the side of the road, guts spilling out and
blood trickling from your twisted mouth. Tire tracks
paved over your once strong body which now
had become flattened into the concrete road.

It must have been dark; the driver must have been
blind to your small shape in the nighttime. Then crash.
Poor Lola, her end came so violently, too rapidly.
My hands became red as her fur stuck to my fingers.
Her collar barely recognizable as it lay beside her.

Oh, my sweet Lola, you were my first companion,
the first to steal my heart and hold it in your
delicate jaw. Your dog bed remains barren, the
scent of your fur still coated into the cushion.

Your morbid death haunts me into my dreams, I cradle
your memory through the night. My sweet Lola, you were
my everything, then you became my inevitable heartbreak.
Your body resides beneath the soil of the abandoned ranch
house, doomed to be buried with the dumped carcasses
of all the other animals who witnessed their doomed
ending upon the cursed land in which we lived upon.

Goodbye Lola, my cherished, precious flower, you
bloomed then evaporated like a shining, falling star.
Disappearing into the blackness of the abyss in the night.

Gidget

There is a ringing in the air, the curious gaze then my hands as they pick up the phone cautiously and bring it to my listening ear. There is a storm gathering outside as the clouds turn black and stinging needles fall from the sky. A haunting presence hangs around me like a looming darkness. You were born on this wretched day, but you blew yourself away and now you are underneath the soil in which you rose from. Memories of my father race into my head and I wonder if this day could become any worse as I tumble through the gloom.

The soft tone of my mother's voice drift through the speaker and she speaks words of death and misery. The sky is screaming now, the winds whistle, and the trees bow down to the chaos that sways their leaves and bends their branches.

My keys are dangling from my hands as I abandon the place in which I work at as a deep sense of dread clutches onto my heart as the car speeds away into the hellish night. The needles crash against my car as the world outside becomes blurry and vague, the images swirling around and melt away into the ground. The clouds hang like demons in the sky, they spit down hateful lights of ruin.

The destination is a mere shadow amid the havoc. The lights are bright in the building and the cold stings my skin. The woman behind the counter has sad eyes and a devastating smile. The dogs which lay shelter in the brick walls yell into the night, the echoes of their yowls bouncing off the walls.

The room in which Gidget lies in is small and suffocating. There is my mother, sitting by the frail and sickly canine as she becomes nothing but hollow bones and dissolving flesh. The scary man enters with the needle of death, his words frightful and his hands unkind as he sticks the needle into the red flesh. The haunting storm raging on the outside pounds at the roof and lashes out at the land around, there is an eerie sensation that prickles my flesh and drops my heart into my stone-hard gut.

Your eyes shut as the needle pushes deeper into your unmoving paw, your shallow breathing ceases and suddenly you are nothing but a bag of bones. Tears flood the room and tremors of sorrow shake the floor beneath us, the tiles containing an icy frost.

Death enters and takes you away, floating you into the darkness of the gale erupting around us. Poor sweet Gidget, she met her gruesome end and sunk into the soil, meeting my ghostly father who holds his hand out on the other side, leading her into an infinite light.

Violet

You were merely a mutt the size of a ball. Your short legs
walked into my vision with your sleek, black coat. Your
teeth sharp as you chased the ball into the endless meadow
of grass. Your paws trailed dirt through the log cabin
floors while you pranced around with your ears flopping.
Your long, furry tail wagged when desirable hands pet
your flesh and scratched at your belly. Your tongue lolled
as you soared across the dirt, yowling through the air.
We were children running through the shining daylight.

Now your muzzle has turned grey, your legs crumble
beneath you as you lie on the floor and sleep soundly.
Your once dark coat now fades into your skin.
Silver white strands poke through your bones.

You make a nest on my bed. My fingers wade through
your soft coat, the unpleasant solitude washing away, you
bring warmth upon my skin and light into my home. You
stay by my side as I soar like a bird away from everybody.
I live in a dream on my own. The spine-chilling wintry
nights become bearable when you lie by my feet with your
loyal eyes and gentle panting. Your velvet fur coats me like
a blanket, you protect me from the ugliness of nightfall.

You followed me while I grew from a tiny caterpillar
into an independent, grown butterfly. Your presence
calms the thunder that rumbles within me, you
put out the fire which seethes onto my flesh.

I keep you safe and give you an extravagant life
until the end of your years comes upon you.

You are my ray of hope in the era of darkness; you are my
light that beams in my life. To passing by peers you are
simply a pet, a meaningless pooch living inside my home.
In my heart, you are my savior. You are my sweet tulip,
glistening like a glorious garden in the season of spring.

Raging Hurricane

She whistled and blew throughout the air, swinging the trees and bushes, making them dance with each other while she flew. She cried out harsh tears, pouring onto the land, swishing, and swirling the soggy ground beneath, releasing the sorrow and pain hidden in her core.

Listen to me! Hear my cries and release me
from this rage tumbling within me!

She roared while her breezy wrath flung her surroundings away, washing out the life and light, twirling the oceans, causing chaos, and disrupting the peace.

There was no living creature left while she corrupted the landscape, raining over the atmosphere. Why should she be the only lonesome soul? She thought despairingly while she tumbled and crashed throughout the grey skies. She spread coldness and disaster everywhere she went.

Her powerful sighs tore the roots of trees from the earth, tossing the bark and ripping away the rough exterior. She let her rage fall deeper upon nature, swallowing the serenity and radiance of the sun, surrounding the once beautiful terrain.

She destroyed homes and brought fire upon the land. She tore the happiness away from the living. Hoping, maybe she would not be alone in her eternal suffering.

II

Little Girl Inside of Me

The little girl inside of me weeps when she is ignored
and cries herself to sleep. The little girl inside of
me yearns for a blazing fire to keep her warm and
a bed filled with animals to keep her safe.

The little girl inside of me wishes for her father's arms
to sweep around her small body but he is nowhere to
be found. She sinks down a dim, despairing hole. The
little girl inside of me pounds on my bones and sinks her
teeth into my skin. She screams at me, then she crawls
back into the dark with defeat weighing her down.

I push the little girl inside of me away and banish her
from my village. She wanders and sobs in the night,
desperately calling out to me but I am far too gone to hear.

The little girl inside of me prays desperately to find a
loving family to accept her but whenever she comes
close, she is consistently let down. The little girl knocks
on my door, pleading to be let inside. I look at her
through the peephole and I proceed to lock the door.

The little girl inside of me sings an ode. She
paces through fog, flying with crows.

She is consumed by the frosty wind. Her bones become icicles, piercing her flesh. Her bare feet bleed from thistles. Ghosts follow her trail; they dig her grave in the chilly winter. In the bleak land, she roams alone. She wears a black veil, floating in the breeze.

She disappears within the shadows of the eerie nightfall.

I am free of her hold. I release her from her pestering pain of abuse and tension. She flies away into the horizon, thanking me for the newfound peace.

The scared girl I used to be died years ago, she burst into flames then rose from the ashes to start anew. The little girl inside of me is gone, her haunting presence is replaced by a woman with the strength of a bull and confidence as high as the sky.

Sailing in the Sea

The boat floats away from the dock and the waves
crash gently against the walls. We sail into the open sea.
You stand there with your bare chest, your black curly
hair blows in the slight breeze of the salty ocean air.

The leech with long hair and tight bathing suit sits
beside you, hanging onto you as if you were her
life jacket. Her son sits beside her, his wide curious
eyes gazing across the horizon of the sea.

I watch the birds dancing across the sky; my hand
falls into the passing water and I swish it around. My
sister leans over the edge and my father snaps at her
viciously. There is a dolphin's fin swaying with the
waves nearby and I beg my father to steer closer, but
he refuses. His attention is pulled away from me by the
leech who touches his arm and whispers in his ear.

Jealousy crashes into me, I feel connected to the hurtling
waves that sway beneath me. There is a yearning inside
of me to leap off my seat and sail away into the sea. I float
with the flow of the ocean, letting it take me into paradise.

He does not need me; he has his leech. She clutches his
bones, pulling him underneath the sea with her, leaving
me behind to navigate on my own in the wild, restless loch.

WHY?

A burning question haunts my mind, especially at night
when I am lying alone in my bed, feeling vulnerable and
violated. Why would you do that to me? An innocent
girl who did not know any better. I see shadows of
your curly black hair dancing across the walls.

Why would you touch me and talk to me like
that? An innocent girl who should have been
treated like a daughter, not a partner or toy.

Why would you ruin me like that? My childhood
was taken from me without my knowledge, my mind
ruined. My sense of boundaries and what is right and
wrong became damaged and broken. Why? Why? Why?
Why would you act like a sick, twisted bastard? Why
couldn't you have just been a normal, healthy father?

Why would you do it? Why would you do it?

Your words act as a puppet show. You pull me
close, convincing me that everything is alright,
convincing me that you are not a monster.
Did you forget the fact that I was just a child?
I did not deserve it. I did not need that. I did not want it.

I look at fathers and daughters and feel a burning jealousy. It is unfair. My blood boils at the thought. Anger and bitterness are all I have; it is all I am made of and it is all your fault.

Why did you have to fuck me over?

I am violated. My relationships are full of distrust and fear. Are they cheating? Are they abandoning me? Do they feel disgusted when they look at me? I crave touch, yet it causes me to crumble into sickness. Every day when the thought of what I went through crosses my mind, I can feel my throat closing. Endless tears spill. I must squeeze them shut and hold my breath.

Strange men will speak vulgar words and compliment my body. I look away and do not respond. A horrid sensation fills me and all I wish to do is run and crawl into a hole. I collapse in on myself like a suffocating avalanche of icy snow.

Nobody will understand if I tell them what is wrong. I am so deeply wounded. There is a swirling storm of emotions inside of me and I fear they will never be set free. I will forever be stuck in a dark turmoil. Forever traumatized, feeling so alone.

You are dead and will never know the pain you caused me. Why did it have to end that way? Why couldn't you have apologized before you left? Coward. Why did you have to be so cruel and neglectful? Why did you have to come on to me like that?

Why? A question which will never have an answer. I am left wondering and feeling sick to my stomach every day with no ending. Why did you spiral? Why did you not want to get better? Why do I blame myself? Why do I have a disgust towards myself, and not you? You are to blame. You are at fault. You were the prowling predator, ripping me apart piece by piece.

Sinister

We sit underneath the lampshade which illuminates
the dark. Your hand slides across my childish
skin, leaving a path of bruises. Your words are
convincing as your tongue speaks a gentle lullaby
of tenderness, you hold me in the palm of your
hand, and you coddle me like a delicate flower.

Your expensive watch shines in the black of the room,
chills creep up my skin into my spine as your hand grips
my thigh, my stomach becomes queasy and my eyes
dart across the quiet room, wondering if I should run.

You coat me with sinister touches; my blood boils as
you dangle me above a fire; the flames dance in my
eyes as they burn my skin. Your eyes are dangerous as
your gaze flies over my frail physique, my breasts still
developing but that does not stop your wandering pupils.

You puncture me with a sharp knife, slicing the edge over
the cuts and leaving them to fester and rot. The wounds
sting as they leave a fiery path on my damaged skin.

The water runs hot and cold on my skin as you creep
into the room and gaze upon my sacred tomb. My
hands are quick, rushing to cover my body. You gaze
upon the sanctuary you know you should not enter
but that does not stop you from peering admiringly.

You hold my hand and tug me towards you, breathing in my scent and holding me as if I were your lover. Your touch is unsettling, but I hear whispers which tell me this is what love is.

Your dark touches follow me into my dreams. I wake in an uncomfortable state, sweat pouring down my skin. My bed turns to an ice-cold lake.

There is something sinister about you; the signs were clear, but I was a mere fawn leaping through a fantasy land of grass-filled meadows. I had a powerful, blind devotion towards you, despite your disturbing touches and vulgar, uneasy comments.

Cigars

You tap your stinging cigar
onto my skin.

Your sinister hands
caress my child-like flesh.

Your fatherly gaze burns holes
into the innocence of my body.
I cover myself with my arms
they act as a see-through shield.

Your gaze does not divert
from my developing breasts
and womanly curves.

Liar

All that pours from your sly mouth are manipulative lies. You only exist in your narcissistic world. I was merely an innocent butterfly. You used your hands to crush me when you were supposed to gently hold me. You play the victim, but you are far from innocent.

You stated you could not visit us because of work, but that was a lie. Little did I know you used that weekend to entangle yourself with a minor for your perverted usage and pleasure. Little did I know you spent your time falling deeper off that cliff and sinking into felonious acts.

My father went away long ago. In his place stood a destructive sinner with a horrible, mind-killing disease of addiction. You were not you but that does not excuse the words you spit out and your heartbreaking actions. The drugs overtook you and swept through your head like a wildfire, leaving nothing but an empty shell and irreversible damage.

When your demise came upon you, you were nothing but a liar with poor excuses and a lifetime's worth of devastation. But you were still my father, despite all the lies that erupted from your lips. Now you are gone. You will never have that chance to redeem yourself because you wanted the easy way out. I do not revere the gory way you chose to break away from the chains.

You truly took your lies to your grave, buried with you in that black coffin beneath the ground.

Where Did You Go?

The time on the clock ticked slowly. We wait in the vacant
parking lot for you to arrive. Time seemed to drag on and
restlessness made its way into the small space of the car.

One minute, ten minutes, thirty minutes, one hour.
You still had not shown up and I slowly started to lose
hope. I realized once again you were not coming.
My mother turned around in her seat. She
defeatedly stared at us. She carried the weight
of disappointment on her shoulders.

"He's not coming."

She spoke the dreadful words that my sisters and I had
been thinking. He is not coming again; he is on a bender.

Once more he prioritized drugs and forgot about
his family, waiting for him to arrive, waiting
for him to be a father. Impatience and agitation
consume me. I ponder over different theories as
to why you are not here again but none of them
cover up the sinful truth that you are not you.

We drive away into the black of the cold
night, dejection hanging in the air above
us like a fish dangling above water.

Hopeful, longing glances at my phone, waiting
for your text but the message never comes,
and my phone screen stays empty.

Where did you go? Why aren't you here? You said you
would be here but that promise you made fell away and
was merely an empty wish and would not come true.

The little girl inside of me is screaming and crying,
wishing her father would be here but little does she
know that you are too far gone into the abyss.

The next time we are supposed to meet in the middle
of South Carolina, you arrive late, and you smell
strongly of cigarettes and something else that I could
not place. My mother said goodbye then drove away,
her car fading into the night, leaving us with my father
who was like a feral and dangerous jungle cat.

You had a crazed look in your eyes that drove
anxious nerves into my prickling skin. The car
began swerving and you seemed out of control,
yet I was powerless in your company.

Your eyes were shutting. You nearly ran us into the side
of the road. Your voice snapped. Fear planted itself onto
me and I sat there helplessly. Your hands shook on the
steering wheel. Death seemed inevitable that night. The car
got too close to the other lane with vehicles driving past us.

Five in the morning finally arrived when
we drove through Florida to the grim ranch
house in the blackness of early dawn.

You could have killed your daughters. Blood
would have stained your hands because of
the drug-induced recklessness that overtook
you. You acted like a chilling stranger.

Oh, father, where did you go? Why have you
been replaced with this hideous, frightful man?
Where did you go? I need you to come back!

I float in the breeze like a lost kite outside of the gate
to your heart. A sinister penumbra hangs above you.
A storm rages: you are blown away like a midnight
star, falling down an oblique cliff. I chase you
through a never-ending, maddening labyrinth.

The Day You Died

There is a grey cloud hanging in the air. The day
becomes dark and the night sweeps in. A dreadful
sensation makes its way into our home, infecting
the air with a pouring storm. I tiptoe around the
halls which lie silent. I wait for my mother to come
crawling out of the shadows where she cowers.

Time ticks on the clock and everything changes.
I am thrown into turmoil, an unfriendly breeze
bangs at the windows; crows soar above my head
and the floor becomes red hot with blood.

The man who took your place sits down on his
newfound throne and calls upon us. There are
silent tears slipping down my mother's red cheeks.
His eyes are mournful and sympathetic; they bore
holes into my skin; I shrink under his gaze.

You speak of the death of my troubled father. There are
moments of silence and I am lifted out of my body and
thrown into the air; I am placed into a dream-like place and
my eyes shut in hopes of waking up to my warm, soft bed.

The words stick themselves onto me and I shake my head, my teeth rattling and my fingers trembling. Stones the size of large rocks fall upon our heads and crush our skulls; we lie on the floor as we are drained of our souls, the truth settles into us and watches as we suffer. The black, deathly crows pick at our skin and trot over our bodies.

"He's not coming back." I crumble underneath the words and collapse into sorrow.

My phone is placed in my hand and I call upon you. One call, no answer. Two calls, no answer. Three then four then five calls. You do not answer, your voice wafts through the air as your voicemail repeats on a cycle in my head. Your voice which will never speak again; your fingers will never hold the phone close to your ear as you talk sweetly to me through the speaker.

I huddle in the corner while a darkness rushes over my body; I rot in my spot and there is a flood pouring down my eyes, raining down onto the floor. I am smashed into the ground, doomed to dwell on the loss of your presence.

My bloodshot eyes dance across the room, following the shadows and I wonder if one of them is you. My body is curled into itself and I fall deeper into sorrow. My bed is made of rocks as my spine cracks and my bones are broken. My mind whirls and sleep does not come that night as it walks away

from me and leaves me to suffer, conscious and
trembling as if my body were an earthquake.

The day you died destroyed everything inside of me.
A plague swept over my family and the sky remained
black for so long. The day you died was horrendous
and grim, but that day passed and now the memory of
your death is vague and the grief for your loss is soft.

You are gone, but life goes on and the darkness
has lifted away to a bright horizon. The day
you died is just that, another ordinary day.

Death

Death creeps around the corners of the halls in the dark
like a ravening lion, following you like a shadow and
taunting you with whispers in your guilty conscience. He
walks among the land, inhaling souls and riding upon a
stallion made of tar, his hooves sparking a path of lava.

You live in that ghastly house with your demons,
walking among the despairing floors with your
head dropping down and your skin wearing
away. Ghosts of your sins hang around your neck,
suffocating you and blowing every breath away.

Death dances around you, waving his sharp dagger
at your heart, tempting your desire to escape.

Death holds your hand while you blow your head away,
blood erupting from your damaged skull, slipping
across the floor of lava pooling into a river of red. Death
cradles your soul while you come to the bitter ending of
your shameful life. Death smiles smugly while he floats
over your mangled body which rots into the ground.

Death speaks sweet words of encouragement into
your ears, telling you to be released from your
prison that you trapped yourself inside of.

You slip into the veil. Too late to be a role model.

Funeral

The coffin lies on the stand; it taunts me with its
haunting presence. The Jewish man rolls blue colors
off his tongue, flooding the room with despair.
Tears run down my red cheeks; your red body
lies in the box, your bones rotting into dust.

They speak nostalgic words and wipe their
eyes. I sink back into the shadows, my grief
engulfing me, setting me on fire. I am hurling
anguish at the faceless bodies around me.

Why must you be gone? Come back and save me
from this eternal pain! Crawl out from that dim
coffin and take me away to a place of sunshine!

The men take you away; the car drives slowly down
the paved road to hell. Your body falls into the soil and
is covered by ash. Stones fall on top of my shoulders
and the wet, slippery tears create a pool in my face.
My mouth fills itself with my tears and there is a rope
pulling tightly at my neck, choking away my shallow
breath. Your body disappears and I crash into misery.
My knees fall apart, and I am a broken corpse. My limbs
scattered around the ground. The wind blows at my
chilled skin and whispers words of comfort in my ear.

My eyes are stitched onto the ground in which you lie. The soil which buried you covers my vision. I am thrown into the chaotic ripples of bittersweet memories. Wretched weeping shakes me to the core.

The trees lift me up and cradle my shivering body. Your body becomes far away until I cannot see you anymore. You have vanished from the living. I am hoisted into the sky and released into the clouds.

I float to a better place, leaving you behind until you are faded into the distance like a falling star.

Father

You are a puzzle which I will never solve. How could I not have known; how could I not have picked up the signs. Deep down I felt a rotten sense of dread. The nights you did not come home. The nights you arrived after I had been put to bed. The nights your seat was left empty and cold at the dinner table. The quiet defeat in my mother's eyes, the tension rising in the air when you were around. You were a chaotic tornado. You swept through our family and left nothing but piles of wreckage. Instead of spending time with family, you were too busy snorting drugs and fondling your work assistants.

There is helplessness in my lungs, I breathe in your suffocating chemicals. Your frigid greed harshly rips away my drooping innocence, throwing my mutilated body into a dim hole.

Your glittering soul is taken by chaos. I am thrown into a maddening tsunami, my body is overcome with lassitude, my lips singing a symphony of insanity.

I walked on fragile eggshells around you, say the wrong thing and I would be roadkill, flattened and kicked away. I could not express myself negatively, in your eyes it was a sign of weakness. You shrieked, becoming an aggressive lion, threatening to pull out the wooden paddle or whack us with your rounded, spiky belt.

Your moods would give me whiplash. They poured down
like rain, disappearing as soon as they came. Unpredictable
and inconsistent. A cycle circling like a Ferris wheel.
All or nothing with you. A white star or a black hole. I
hide in the corner, a blank stare, traveling to a fantasy
world in my head to tune out the chaos and arguments.

Fear drove my actions. Keep quiet or speak up?

A memory often comes up out of the dark where you
and my mother are fighting, bleeding screams from your
mouths and blazing fire in your eyes. I am sitting in the
corner of the kitchen and fearfully watching. I thought you
would hurt her because of the intensity of your aggression.

I still felt loyal towards you. I yearned for the sounds
of your dangling keys in the door, coming back to your
family. Most nights it did not happen, and I would go to
bed feeling cold and abandoned. Memories of you when
I was young seem faded and far, I try to reach them, but
they float away like balloons. Gone within seconds.

The divorce was messy and hectic. You moved out
into your beach house. My mother and my siblings
stayed in the ranch house filled with ghosts. My
sisters and I visited you on weekends and you
would smell of cigarette smoke and weed.

You and my mother would yell and claw at each other outside of the car in parking lots when you came to drop us off or pick us up. You began expressing your sexual side and making vulgar comments around us, merely innocent children. In your eyes, we were puppets. Controlling us, manipulating us.

You introduced us to her. The woman in her twenties with a seven-year-old son. She had long, dark hair and suggestive clothing with her breasts peeking out from her tight clothes. She smelled like you. Cigarettes floating around her.

She was the leach that stuck onto you and tore the family apart. You had affairs with her when I was too young to know but my mother kept the disgusting secret for years. You loved younger women; they turned you on and brought out your perverted side.

On my tenth birthday, you promised you would make it home to spend time with me. You never did. My mother took me out shopping then stopped by your office late at night to surprise you with your daughter. She told me to wait in the car, which I did obediently. My mother was gone for ten minutes, then fifteen, then twenty.

I was wondering what happened and telling myself I should go inside, then she came back and seemed agitated. My mother told me you could not see me right now, then she sped off with me. I felt dejected and blue. All I wanted was to see my father on my first double digit birthday. Doesn't he love me? Why would he cower in hiding?

Summer came upon us, my mother informed me we were moving to a faraway land. We packed up everything, then vanished to North Carolina. You moved back into the ranch house and picked up your business of breeding Arabian horses. I looked back through the trunk window, emptiness consuming me while I watched the house become smaller in the distance. Our long dead German Shepherd chasing us, then falling into dust. We left you behind. You threw yourself into turmoil.

You spiraled further into drugs and the woman with her little boy. We drove halfway to South Carolina every other weekend to meet you, then you would drive the rest of the way to the ranch house filled with despair. You were moodier after the move, there was a wild look in your eyes. You exposed us to a darker side of yourself.

You lied, telling us the goats had found good homes. Our mother told us the truth of your idea to send those innocent animals to a slaughterhouse, for them to be killed and tossed away as if they were nothing. Your lack of humanity tears me apart.

You became openly sexual with the leech. Boundaries were now non-existent between you and your daughters.

I would wake up early, excited to spend time with my father but then discover I had to wait two, three, sometimes four hours for you to exit your room and come out into the open. You and the woman would spend so much time in that bedroom and I, an innocent girl, had no idea of the erotic and illicit activities that went on.

Jealousy consumed me. I yearned for your attention. When she was not around, I got my wish in a way which made me feel disgusting.

My body was an object that you could stare at for pleasure. We were pawns in your corrupt mind, ruined by the influence of the drugs which you loved to snort and ingest.

There were demons in my mind throwing rotten thoughts into my head. That woman and the drugs must have been more important for you to often check out and walk away from your daughters; they must have been a better choice than spending time with your family, maybe we just were not enough.

Maybe the light died out inside of you and all you could do was bury yourself in bad choices and shady actions. You were gone, first came the death of your mentality, then came the disappearance of your presence. No longer did I expect to see you, then eventually all ties were cut, and the connections fell.

You destroyed our family; you tore away from
communication and because of your drug-induced
personality you took away your support for us.
We had to pack up our belongings again to move
into a rental house. My poor mother could not
afford our house anymore because of you.

Questions poured through me and insecurities
seeped into my veins because of your neglect. Didn't
you care for us anymore, were we dead to you?

I will never know. You chose to blow your head away
in that dreadful log cabin with drugs stuffed in the
corners. The guilt gnawed through your flesh into the
bone. You heart became infected with tar-filled goo.

My father, a treacherous man. My father, a victim of crime.
My father, the man who was supposed to be my protector.
But instead, brought ruinous damage upon my soul.
Yet forgiveness finds its way into my heart. The drugs
which controlled you and the narcissism which consumed
you had revealed your dark side. They swallowed
you, until you were merely an empty shell of a man.

You had not been yourself for a long time.
In the future, I stand in your place. Darkness
surrounding my space. I breathe madness and inhale
capsules. My mentality shattering like glass.

I understand. No longer in control, the brain a foggy storm.

The difference between you and I, is that I escaped from the chains of lunacy. I changed. I got better. I made amends and walked away from my impending doom.

Never Good Enough

Knowing that what you do is not good enough cuts
deep to the core, tearing open your skin to leave you
bleeding out and gagging on your own breath.

You try to impress others and do things you normally
would not do, but it is never enough. You plan desperate
acts and shout out, but they cannot hear you and you
are falling further into the dark. "Look at me! Love
me!" What do I have to do for you to notice? You paint
a canvas of lies over yourself in a desperate attempt to
get them to stay, to feel loved and needed because, in
the end, it drives you into madness and deception.

They always want more.

The wretched sensation of fear hangs on tightly,
whispering that one day they will decide they do not
need you anymore. You will be kicked to the curb and
ran over, squashed and rotting on the side. There is
someone better, you are not doing enough. Work harder!
Your energy is lost, and you fall behind because, in the
end, there is only so much you could do. "Do more"
they say! You cannot because your words are caught.
Your limbs are dangling from your helpless body and
the strength withers until you are glued to the ground.

When they come crawling back, begging for your
forgiveness, you forgive them because you do not want

them to feel the same pain and rejection that they gave you. You are so afraid of the haunting loneliness that you put them before yourself and you lose yourself to codependency and giving too much. Eventually, you run out of love and you are drained of everything.

You try to see the beauty and the positive in everything, picking apart the ugly flaws and separating them from the good. But it does not work. You will always find something wrong, something not quite right. It tears you down and rips you open, exposing everything. The insanity claws at your skin and you find yourself stumbling and itching for approval. When they talk down and deceive you, you are suddenly shattering and folding in on yourself. The negative beats down the optimism. You can no longer reach the light which has become dim.

Whenever you try to get back up, insecurities cause you to fall back down and the fear consumes you until you are paralyzed. "They're leaving. They're finding someone new."

It messes with your mind and it causes you to wonder if what you did was ever good enough. "You're nothing."

You know no matter how hard you try, no matter how many times you change for the wrong people, it'll just never be good enough and you're stuck in a cycle of trying then falling and crumbling, then getting back up and resetting, doing the same thing over and over again every day until you have faded from reality.

Fantasy

In my mind
you are a mighty king.

Realistically
you are a scared boy
running from your fears
playing hide and seek
in the dark.

Empty Promises

Your crumbling words
shatter
like glass
tearing my heart
crushing my lungs.

Your mouth rots
it tells tales
of disappointment.

My bones break.

A heavy stone
drops in my gut.

You hold a knife
to my throat.

Your promises
mean nothing
they are tossed away
like broken toys.

Endless tears spilled.

Look the Other Way

I called out in times of darkness.
You came by, your voice wondering.
You heard my mournful cries
then looked the other way.

Crawling maggots
gnaw at my veins.

Your elusive soul
is an illusive concept.

I hopelessly chase you
for your approval.

Grotesque vines entangle
your decrepit heart.

You willingly stroll
past the sylvan veil
into the pits of hell
disregarding my pleas
vanishing like cascading lilies.

You left the door open
for lurkers of nightfall
to wander inside.

Trapped

The room is a tight cage. My feet take me back and
forth like a hungry tiger. My hands shake, my claws
itch to attack. The snarl on my face twists agitatedly.
My head hung low, with nowhere to go. Backed into a
corner, my legs bring me forth, I trample the innocent.
Back and forth. Back and forth. There is a quick
pace in my step. My eyes blaze like a lion,
the hair on my skin prickling like a cat.

The fire burns hotly while the tension rises in the air.
I prowl among the streets, the people closing their
blinds while they peer fearfully. Steam rises from the
soil while my feet slide forward, making a fiery path
along the land. Thunder roars and chaos erupts.
I fall towards the edge; the rocks slip beneath my feet.

"Get away!" They yell. "Snap out of it!"

Too late, the air swings around me.
I am a plane crash landing.

I Miss You

You created a mess and did not bother repairing the damage. You showed crude behavior. Blood covers your hands. You tore apart our flesh and ripped into our hearts. The void of losing a fatherly role model nips at my heart.

I miss you before the ravaging virus infected your mind. Before you drowned in indented waters. Before the chains dragged you into the trenches.

You were my savior. You were a loving father. I was a little sparrow, your arm cradling my silky soft skin.

I miss your voice which was music to my ears. I miss your comforting smell of cologne; I miss your knowledge on life and your lectures about business and how to thrive in life. I miss seeing your broad body and gelled, curly black hair. I miss the weekends I would come and visit you. You would be there, waiting by the car, holding out your arms. I miss the rare days you were sober, the days we would get along, the days when you knew what boundaries meant.

I watch childhood videos; I see you and smile. There were better days, there were days I was merely a baby in your eyes. Nothing more. I cannot recall the memories of my younger self. I wish I could recall my early years, and your kindness. All I have are vague flashes. There is a black hole where memories of you should be.

The thought of you lying in your own blood in that grim

house brings tears to my eyes and a choking feeling in my throat. You did not deserve to die alone in such a spine-chilling manner. I see movies and characters that blow their own heads off and I wonder if that is what you looked like when you made the choice to end your life. Was it merely a quiet bullet that went into your head, or was it messy with your head exploding off your body? I shake those thoughts away because the feeling of bile rises in my throat at the mere image of it.

I miss you and you have vanished into
the air, gone like a leaf in the wind.

Sand Between My Feet

The beach is quiet and the sand tickles my feet, the
harshness of the soil burning my skin. The water
tumbles slowly, the waves crashing against the damp
dirt; sparks of light shine off the ripples in the sea.
The wind blows a breeze through my golden-brown
mane which hangs around my head elegantly.

Seagulls soar across the turquoise sea. I watch
with speechless wonder while the crepuscular
moon comforts my burning soul. A fugacious
sense of tranquility consumes my mind.
Footprints of love fade into the sand.
Night fallen echoes whisper in the wind.

The memory of my father is distant. His curly, black hair
swings in the breeze, his hands caressing my face as he
slithers like a snake around me. The sand pulls him under,
his presence evaporates, and solitude overcomes me.

I walk with sand between my pale feet, breathing
in the salty air and closing my eyes.
I float through the tumbling ocean away from splintered
disdain. I discover a pyrrhic victory & gleaming rainbows.

An aromatic petrichor drifts in the quiet stillness
of the breeze, erasing the rotting scent of burning
corpses. Emollient begonia's graze my flesh

A smile turns my lips upward. I know an endless wonderland is coming towards me. I dance with the dolphins and soar with the doves circling the fluffy, white clouds.

Farewell

Your voice is a warm lullaby
your rough hand securely holding mine
your arms embracing me.

Never again shall I enter the log cabin
and see your curly black hair,
feeling at home
while you make bacon and eggs.

You have fallen into the dust
your remnants blown away.
Your green eyes
become holes
in your face.

Goodbye father,
your memory is cherished,
even when you were not at your best.

All is forgiven.
I lie down to rest,
knowing that you reside above me,
keeping me safe.

You watch me grow
into the woman
you wanted me to be.

You Live On

I see you in the thickness of my hair.
I see you in the shadow of the night.
I see you in the size of my nose
and the color of my eyes.

You are a part of me
you live on in my blood.

Your face
burned into my head.

You live on
as a man,
the first to steal my heart
carrying me upon your shoulders.

In memory,
a loving father,
the stone reads.

A wilting flower
sits upon the soil
above where you reside.

You live on
in my heart
always.

The abandoned log cabin. A rainbow; a symbol of hope after the death of my father.

My family and me. A forgotten memory, the beginning of a chaotic era. The first three horses we owned. Buzzy, Big Blue and Keyahna (one of our first Arabians; the beginning of a breeding business. The beginning of the ranch house. The beginning of a butterfly effect.)

III

Fly Away

Red robins sit on the windowsill, they sing tunes in
honor of our love. We listen to the sound of each other's
delicate heartbeats. We sink into the tranquil nightfall.

The darkling cloud diminishes when you are around.

You save me from the edge of the cliff,
pulling me back and bandaging me up.

Was it too much?
A day came, your eyes sagged, your lungs fell apart.
We sit on the bed together, you take my sheets
and leave in the chilly dusk.

Your car drives off. I watch helplessly,
your taillights fading
like a twinkling falling star.

Now the birds migrate, the plants rot.
I wait by the window
but you do not return.

I see an omen
blacker than a raven.

A scarecrow
pecking at a rotting corpse
the bones crumbling into ash.

I see my reflection
in the lightless eyes
I see my doom.

Waiting
until death.

When the Sun Goes Down

When thou shalt slumber,
my darkling cloud
comes whirling in the nightfall.

Thunder and lightning
bleeds through the cracks of night.

When the city lights burn away
and the breeze drifts among the bony trees
a moon sea darkness arrives
engulfing my heart.

A ghostly figure
following me
coaxing me
towards the dark mist
of suffocating waves.

We Broke Each Other

The warmth of July brought soft clouds and sunny
days upon me. We left the world and traveled
to the planet of Venus. I was a newly grown
sunflower in your world of darkness and chaos.
We were a tight embrace of gentle touches.

I kissed your skin and acted like a lost puppy that
you could take pity on. You took me in and fed my
grumbling stomach; you affectionately caressed my
skin and placed sloppy kisses upon my tingling lips.

The coldness of October brought a passionate love.
We snuggled underneath the sheets, desperate to shut
out the rotten wintry sensations. There were visions of
growing old in the blur of our life and settling down
in a house. We became lost in our fantasy land.

December brought sharp thistles and torn hearts.
You fell into an abyss of delusions and emptiness
which consumed your shell of stone.

I only meant to love you with a fiery intensity
to wash away your worries filled with vileness.
I only meant to heal your wounds. Instead, I cut
them open deeper and stung your heart.
The flames burned out and your flesh became
scorched. The fire spread into an uncontrollable
stallion. I melted into ash; you escaped my
tightly wound love which suffocated you.

Our age of starlight dissolves. Our stardust
souls rip apart, falling into dark matter. The ebb
and flow of our honeydew passion fades into
a freezing void. Galaxies perish in our vision.
Our hearts transform into a white dwarf.

Venom has tainted the red roses which wafted
through the halls. A reflection of a doomed
passion. Everything eventually ends.

Break My Bones

We sat at the edge of a cliff.
You took my hand,
saying, "jump with me."

I leapt; you stayed.
I crashed into stones,
my blood staining
your hands.

You broke my bones.
You cut my skin.
Your gaze burned.

I enjoyed the wax
running down my flesh.

The rocks
are painted red.
You wipe
them clean.
You bury
my mangled corpse.

There is no eulogy.
You wipe your hands
and dance upon my grave
of deathly sorrow.

Gone

The emptiness
which consumes my soul
is banished from my castle
when you are here.

You vanish
into the cold air.

I am once again
doomed to despair.

Forever Floated Away

You arrive fleetingly
like a migrating Columbidae
singing songs of wonder
in my listening ears.

The insanity
which claws at my flesh
in the darkness
is shunned
into a dusty corner.

We promised each other forever
but that shrank into a rotting flower.
A fire burned within you,
engulfing my bones and turning me to ash.

You poured my remnants into a tin box
then you let it float
down the rippling stream.

We once swam in a refreshing lake
with swans floating around us.
The pond of paradise became red
and charred with coal,
throwing me back into turmoil.

Where was our forever?
You walked out the door
with a match and lighter
in your palm.

No goodbye
from your lips.

I lay upon the kitchen floor,
watching as flames raced around me,
burning our forever and washing it away.

My heart blackened
from your seething
bitterness.

Doe

I race across your path
like a wide-eyed doe.

You hit me
with your carriage
of death.

My guts spill out.
My blood pools
around your feet.

You glance
at the wreckage.
You drive into the silence
of the night.
Your taillights fade
into the dusk.

I am mangled and broken,
devoid of your love.

Loss

Is there any easy way to say goodbye?

Unopened letters.
Voicemails collecting dust
in their phones.
Sorrowful last glances.

All you can say is
I love you
I need you
hoping that it is enough.

Lovers die.
Parents fade into the dust.
Friendships are stomped
into the ground.
Hearts are ripped out.

Their bones
will sink into the soil.
Their ears
listening
to squawking crows.

Speak the truth
or choose to live a life
of eternal silence
filled with solitude.

Dancing Flowers

The garden we visit is exquisite. The sun glistens above us, the flowers sway in the breeze. Red apples hang above us, the stems hung low on the tree. You pluck a rose, a finger trails my hair, tenderness escaping from your touch. A strawberry in your hands, the juices of the ruby red fruit slip down your mouth upon my own.

Irises twirl in my vision; roses are planted upon my skin. We float along the colorful pathway into the land of beauty. Your eyes resemble the brightness of the light; I am a flower and I breathe in your cedar, glowing like the sun. Flowers dance at my feet, carrying me upon their petals.

The sunset in the horizon paints my skin and warms my heart, you sweep me further into the enchanting garden. You place a crown upon my head. You kiss my hand, your lips soft like peonies.

Dandelions bloom in honor of our idyllic love, the flowers bow down to us. You gaze upon me. I am a radiating star in your presence. You set me up on a canvas amid the flowers, painting me with marvelous, warm colors and coating my skin with lilacs.

The garden goes on, endless pavements and rows of trees with fruits holding the stems of leaves. We stroll into the middle, sunflowers all around. Your tender kiss upon my pink lips, the squeeze of your rough hands. Then came the coldness of your disappearance. I stand among the garden with flowers dancing in the wind, mocking my sorrow.

There was once blossoms on the trees. There was a fragrance of marigolds drifting in the wind. Ashen clouds absorb the warmth of spring. I stand alone in the deathly winter, weeping in the solitude. The tree turning into bones. Rose petals transform into brittle twigs

I walk through ivory orchids in a midnight garden. I search for your love amidst the dancing, fading flowers. They taunt me with your haunting memory, along with the rotting fruit on the shadowy trees.

The deathly silence is a vicious reminder
of the cold emptiness of loss.

Eerie

A decaying cabin sits upon the rotting grass, speaking
secretive tales. The cracked path remains empty, nobody
dares to roam near the ghastly building. Streaks of
blood stain the walls, the front door left wide open.

Vines entangle the exterior. The teapot
whistles, water floods the faded tiles.
Crows sit upon the roof, screaming songs of
loneliness while eerie clouds stroll by.

Seasons Change

Our devotion had been passionate
like embers and flames.
The fire grew small
then died out.

A wintry dusk
swept over the rolling hills
of evergreen grass.

My intuition spoke extrinsic whispers
that our red streaked love
would disappear into gloomy skies.

Our quixotic connection recoiled like a snake.
Poison seeped into our blood,
squashing our elysian twilight love.

Gold tulips rot.
Nights of musical tunes evaporated.
In their place came silence in nightfall.

The birds went quiet
and the sun went down.

A black hole
consumed the bright stars
shining in your eyes.

I lay amongst barren trees.
I sink into the darkened dirt.

You plant a stone
in memory of our love.

Your shape retreated
fading into the night
like a ghost
disappearing from my life.

You never looked back.

Running Away

You tighten the reins
on your heart
galloping away.

You are a prickly cactus
cutting open
my burning
fragile flesh.

You switch
the channels
from romance
to horror.

Your hands play
with my soul
too close
then too far.

You are gone.

No Escape

The moon high in the sky
observing inhabitants
resting beneath her.

A woman
frantic
while she runs.

A man
behind her
chasing
as if she were a rat
and he is a cat.

The road is empty.
Ghosts float
beneath the sky.

A wail is heard.
Candles are blown out
in windowsills.

The rippling creek is calm,
oblivious to the blood
staining the grass
pooling around the fallen leaves
disappearing into the fog.

Mourning

She sits by the rippling stream,
ashes floating into the tides,
a faded photograph clutched in her hand.

If she takes a breath from her weeping
she would see the silhouette
of a man standing beside her
his hand on her shoulder
he acts as her guardian.

The sun sets.

The woman wipes her tears
then wanders back to her empty cabin
filled with sentimental memories
and a newly unoccupied bed.

The left side of her sheets collects dust.

Amongst Shadows

I wish to escape
from these chains of misery.
I wish to no longer
be a daughter of shame.
I wish to erase my sins
and begin anew.

I bear a weight
of a thousand stones.
I drown underneath
the deafening silences
of heartbreaking regrets.

I am haunted
by sunken memories
and blurry silhouettes
of death.

Alone

Thorns entangle the cactus.

Dust rolls by
engulfing inhabitants
of the desert.

The scorched sun
burns the sand
until fire rises from the soil.

The lone cactus
weeps softly.

Nobody dares to love her.

Nobody wishes
to caress
her prickly skin.

Dark Love

I make a den with the darkling crow.
He entangles me with his soft feathers.
We soar into the sky with each other.

A radiating luxurious passion.

His eyes become
beady and black.

His talons are sharp
piercing my heart.

His beak
spits out
vile language.

He soars away
leaving me
in a nest of sorrow.

His mysterious soul intrigues me.

My curiosity was my downfall.

String Me Along Like A Puppet

My skin shredded into thin paper; my
bones withered into thorns.
Is it your love that I crave in the deadly
silence of the chilling night?
You were like no other, you brought luxurious
gifts upon my empty nest. You brought
soft caresses within gentle wings.
Your edges are rough like a stone and your
memory hangs above me like a heavy weight.
Your soft spot is hidden in the depth of your blank
pages. You may be a tin man but there is hope in
your metallic heart as your blood runs cold.

I flutter around you like a butterfly, my colors sending
vibrant tenderness through you. You captured me within
rough velvety hands. You lock me in a cage, keeping me
contained while you stare and prod for your pleasure.

The eggs in my nest are gone. The colors have faded
to a blackest hue. You toss me into the frigid air.
You stole my love and never gave it back; now I am
barren like winter and sorrowful like a crow.

I pluck petals off sunflowers, hoping for a time
to come for you to glance at my hopeful gaze
and remember our powerful connection.

You Left

We sit on the bench of love. The bus arrives, the time ticks.
You stand, tip your hat while you wave your hand. You
stroll onto the bus, leaving me behind to wander astray.

Slipshod thoughts tear me apart. There is no
panacea for your rotten heart. My sweetheart
departs, a giant hole fills my soul.

An eclipse rises in the twilight dusk. Curtains
fall, clock strikes midnight. Our chimera ends.
A scarlet rain of sighs escapes my lips.

I fly away into silky lilies. I shatter your memory
with no resistance, no restraint. I am free.

You perish and I flourish.

Anger

A raging, swirling storm inside of me. A pulsating inferno
builds and rises, hovering at the edge of my flesh like a
wave intent on crashing. I swallow tightly and push it
back down, willing it to go back into hiding and never
show its ugly and foul self. I fight back harsh words,
clench my fists, and squeeze my eyes shut. Breathe
in and breathe out. Hide behind the painted lies.

My body is an earthquake, trembling
with heat, an uncontrollable fire.

The anger can be an invisible, small, scared child.
But it can also become a deafening hurricane.

My face twists with a dark rage. I am a monster and the
remnants of my true self evaporate into the bleak nightfall.

It is an out of body experience. I hear myself screaming
on the inside, a pleading voice yearning for me to stop,
but the anger is consuming, and all hope has left. It is
lashing out at anybody in the path of my destruction,
transforming me into an atrocious being with no mercy.

Anger is a powerful untamed stallion. It is a
terrible disease that latches on. It is sitting on the
border of ruination, my feet swinging helplessly
over the edge. It is an oncoming train which
crashes into me, autopilot takes over.

Relationships are ripped away from me,
tossed into the distance. The anger watches
gleefully while I suffer from the intensity.

I shatter underneath a resentment towards myself.
I let it out on my peers because god forbid, I
let myself take the blame and beatings.

Once the damage is done, the anger crawls
back into my flesh. I am the victim of my own
destruction. It laughs in the background. I struggle
with the consequences of what it did and said.

It is a vicious cycle, one that ruins me
and everything around me.

Why Didn't You Talk to Me?

You did not say hello to me, why didn't you say hello?
You repeatedly say hello every day, but you did not
today. My mind whirls: panic rises within me.

They are abandoning me. I am not good enough.

The words weigh me down like a thousand rocks. I
crumble and crash, melting into lava. I rush to leave
them first before they can utter the terrifying words and
leave me. My defense rises and an intense, furious, and
distressful sensation engulfs my body. The memory of
my father tossing me away like a used doll takes over my
mind. I float on a cloud of delusion. The line separating
imagination and reality becomes a blur, until it snaps.

I try to ignore the rushing voices in my head, but
they are brutal and grueling. I attempt recalling the
times they talked to me, reassured me, made me
feel so merry. But my memory is blank, and it feels
cold and rotten. There is no warmth and it feels
as if those glorious and assuring memories never
happened. It has always been barren and dark.

I do not look at them. I do not talk to them.

*They deserve this. They did not say
anything to me. They hate me.*

The words creep into my brain like a sinister ghost whispering into my ear, forcing me believe them. My teeth grind together. Tears clot my eyes. I realize that I have lost them for what seems like the millionth time.

"Hey."

My heart leaps, I feel whole again.

It continues. They talk to me; I feel joyous and amazed. They ignore me, I crumble and fall. I retreat into the shadows, believing they no longer need me. I idealize suicide because it seems better than being abandoned by the person who has stolen my fragile heart and soul.

Absence of Memories

"What's your fondest or earliest
memory from your childhood?"

The question lingers in my mind and hovers around
me like a darkness that I do not want to acknowledge.
There is a blank void where my memory should be,
and I cannot recall anything that has happened.

What happened during my childhood? Did I
have a childhood? I cannot remember anything!
All the memories are mixed and hazy!

Yesterday is gone, tomorrow is unknown. The disoriented
fog has surrounded all that was, all that is. On the other
side of memory, the little girl inside of me huddles in
the dust. She keeps my memories in a chained box. I am
reaching for truth, for an identity. It slips and I crash.

The pieces of my memory are scattered in the
wind. The puzzle may never be solved, and the
memories stay hidden in the shadows.

"I don't know." I whisper to myself helplessly as I sit
there, gnawing at my lip, unable to recall anything
and being stuck in an endless hole of uncertainty.

People are made from memories. Personalities are carved
from people's experiences in life. But my past is unknown,
my memories are fragile and pass by me quickly.

Uncertainty and doubt cloud my mind. Images creep into my mind and I wonder if it happened, or if it is just my mind making things up to fill in the blank spaces. All things familiar has disappeared.

Often, a burning question haunts: Am I even real?

Come Back

You were not here today, just like the day before. Then
the day before that. You are never here anymore but you
should be. I stand there, twiddling my thumbs. I wait
for you to walk into the door like nothing happened.

I am left wondering where you are
and if you will ever return.

I wonder if the last time I saw you would be the
last. Oh, how I wish I would have appreciated
the last moment of your presence more. But now
my memory is fading, and everything seems
so far. I wonder if I even cross your mind.

I stand there, my heart breaking and tears forming
in my eyes. I stand where you once stood and
replay bittersweet memories in my mind. I try to
keep it together, but it is so hard when I am so
close to falling apart and screaming out in pain.

I yearn for those days where you would arrive,
and I would feel extravagantly happy. I miss
the days where I felt like I could breathe. You
are my oxygen and my strength. I feel like I am
decaying like a living corpse without you here.

All I want is for you to come back and be here, but
it is not happening. Every day I fill myself with false
hope as I keep darting my crazed and sorrowful eyes
towards the door, waiting to catch a glimpse of you.

I stand there with a choking and tight feeling in my hollow chest forming as I realize you are not coming.

It is cold and obscure in the atmosphere. A strange void has filled your presence and I long for you to return to take the darkness away. To wake me up from this horrid nightmare that I am living.

Days go by and I lose my appetite. I cry myself to sleep. I remember your sweet, warm presence. I try so hard to forget about it and move on, but that will not happen.

I make futile attempts to believe that you will be back. You always come back. I hear whispers of gossip from the lips of my family saying that you will not be back this time. My heart shatters to pieces every time I hear those poisonous words.

It replays in my head like demons whispering tauntingly into my ear. He is not coming back. He is gone for good this time.

Just once more I wish to see your face and hear your voice, to feel your skin and merely be around you and feel so safe and secure. I long to talk to you once more and hear your laugh and see your radiant smile. I yearn to be engulfed with a fatherly presence once more.

You are a ghost and I am haunted by how you used to be here.

I am fading and shriveling without you. All I want: for you to be here by my side. I am trying to cling onto the small spark of hope that it will happen, but I am slowly losing that faith.

Once that faith slips, I will break. Once I break, there will not be a recovery. I will be shattered like glass that cannot be fixed. Everything will be alright, even during all the chaos and stress, if you are here with me. But that is not happening, and it is slowly ripping me apart until I am nothing.

Junkie

I curl into a ball as tight as a roll of yarn. The cold, hard wall stabs my back. There are pills scattered on the counter. My hands ball into fists with the capsules teasing my fingers. One pill, two pills, four pills. My throat is scratchy as they shuffle down, releasing me from the despairing pain which consumes me entirely.

More, one is never enough, there is an itch tumbling inside of me to fall into the darkness. It yanks me down further, searching for a cure to this endless suffering. The bottle is empty and there are wondering eyes which follow me through the day. My feet pace the floors; my skin is red hot and there is a wildness in the depths of my soul. Desperation kicks me down. Screams tear at my throat. There is a prickling in my skin, longing for my rescuer. More. More. I need more. All I wish is to be numb. All I wish is to be free of the pain, of the mind consuming guilt.

The capsules call for me in the dark. I try to deny my need, I try to tell them no. My attempts are weak, I fall victim to a twisted cycle.

Fire burns my skin, the pills race away from my grip. You stand there with your arms open, an invitation for my ill-minded heart. The pills are gone. You take their place. There is a yearning for your attention, a strong rope pulls my helpless body towards you. I am sucked

into your chemical breath. My hands grip you with a
horrendous intensity. I bring chaos upon your kingdom.
I am desperate for your touch, to feel safe and secure.

You slowly walk backwards.

Come back! Do not leave! I am overcome with recklessness.
I am a junkie for your love and the sweet citrus which
falls from your lips. My stomach eats itself from the
inside out and my lungs rot when you are not around.

I am afraid of solitude. It is in the deadly blackness
of the night when my demons crawl out. It is when I
am alone in the stillness of the moon when I collapse.
The walls close in on me, the air suffocates me, the
convincing voices become a booming thunderstorm.

To strangers, I am a beast who has escaped and begins
to savagely roam around, my eyes hungry and my claws
ready to attack. There is a restless jiggle in my legs, they
take me further down the pit of desperation and lunacy.
My hands grasping in the dark for anything to keep me
from plummeting underneath the blackness of the ocean,
sinking into my own destruction carved from my hands.

Shadows in the Rain

Rain drips onto the windshield.

Clouds darken the wintry sky.

My wipers go back and forth
back and forth.

If I look closely
the silhouette of my father
follows my path
like a sinister spirit
haunting me
into the bitter nightfall.

Without You

You set me afloat in the vast, blue sea. You ignited
the engine and turned away, leaving me to fend
for myself in the darkness of the trenches. I lack
a fatherly warmth to coat me with blankets.

My skin turns to ice from the chilling tides. I wander
towards the unknown ocean of swirling blackness.
Boats pass by me and snap photos. They see a lost
little girl, sailing through the sea with nobody by her
side. I float within saltwater blues, swimming with
the sharks. I find solace in the cold trenches. I breathe
sadness. I wish to travel through time to a happier era.

Dark

The brightness of the atmosphere has packed its bags and abandoned me. Everything is dim and black. The clouds are grey, and the sky is foggy. There are blank spots and hazy, vague images passing by in a blur.

The future is a gaping, unknown abyss. I am slowly losing hope. Time is either too slow or too fast. I am breathing silence. I beg the shadows to forgive me for my sins.

People ask how I would describe myself and I say ambitionless; the words slip so easily off my tongue. There is a grim fogginess surrounding me, blocking my vision. Blood drips from my fingers, marks make their way across the walls.

The light is slipping from my fingertips like a slippery glass that I cannot hold on to. It is all falling apart and all I can do is watch sorrowfully. I try and fix the light, but it went out years ago.

The sun wears a veil and the dusky midnight lasts forever. I drown underneath suffocating waves. I listen to a nefarious symphony. I watch deathly comets fall from the starlit sky. Fiery sparks explode. My callous heart holds depraved dark lullabies. I slowly slip into a haze of unnerving madness.

I pray for doves of light to soar into my vision.

In a land of beauty and desire, I stand alone. I become a void. I dig my grave with no hesitation. I leave no trace. I sink beneath tar.

I fall and shatter onto the stones. Splat. My bones crack. My blood creates a pool around me, lying in my own destruction.

Winter

I am a restless bear trapped in a small, locked box. I am lost within the pale moon, surrounded by concrete tombs. Wretched skeletons blend into my faded shadow. They spit words, they slash swords. I bathe in blood. I am consumed by thunder and lighting.

The cold air rains down on my chilled skin; my bones transform into icicles. My eyes are frozen shut. I stumble around in the dark, desperately reaching for anything to ground me into reality.

When I stand amid faceless peers and chaotic noise, the swarming bees fly away. The incessant buzzing lowers to a whisper. I drive home falling into isolation. It all goes quiet, the silent blackness returns.

My soul that used to be filled with warmth is barren; snow covers the doorway to the fresh, open air. Flashbacks scratch at my head, driving me up the wall. The corner is my haven as I cradle myself against the blank wall; screams of agony tear at my throat.

Loneliness grips me tightly. I pace the floors; the blackness of the season brings out the coldest sensations which hide in the shadows. Madness swirls around me like a raging, howling storm. Winter is fierce. It drags me through hell, scraping my body on stones and thorns. Blood trails behind me, leaking from my torn skin.

Winter is the season when the lights become dim, then goes out altogether. Blizzards tear through my shelter, destroying the gates and causing havoc upon my fragile skull. Dead trees hover above me, their shadows like bony hands waiting to grip my throat and end the wintry nightmare.

Nights become restless. My skin trembles from the bitter iciness. There is a heavy yearning for a lover to keep me warm but there is a stony solitude all around me. There is no end in this doomed era.

"Can anybody hear me?" I scream into the night, but it is a hopeless cry. The blizzard tunes out my fragile voice.

Winter is unforgiving. I walk into darkness. There is no going back.

Disappointment

All you are is a disappointment with your uncaring gaze and quiet lips; all you are is a disappointment with your sweet, friendly words towards strangers and your sudden silence forced upon me.

You act carelessly; disappointment bubbles within my skin, burning my heart.

You used to hold me high, giving me the world and bowing down at my feet. Now your hands are full of coal while you toss me away, coldness in your sunken heart.

Your bittersweet promises flutter hopelessly into the sky, the sun fades and your words rot. You have foolish notions of what it means to love, of what it means to care.

You hide within walls and locked boxes. Your demeanor is unknown, and your expression is blank.

Disappointment whispers tauntingly in the rumbling breeze. It takes my hand, leading me into an abyss of sorrow. You have vanished into thin air. You are far away; your absence is a disappointment. There is a frown etched upon my agitated face.

All you are is a disappointment, perhaps that is the reason you bolted into the darkness and never looked back. You are a disappointment and you know it was your downfall.

Regret

I am invaded by a persistent parasite swimming in my blood. I fill myself with empty wishes of creating a time machine to revisit my dreaded mistakes. Time travel does not exist, and that realization tears me apart.

The shame builds until it breaks me down to pieces, eating me from the inside out. *It is my fault! I should have done better! I am a disgrace!* Bouncing thoughts taunt me. Stinging rain pounds onto my exposed flesh.

Would things be different if I had chosen to walk down a different path? Is there any right or wrong path? Conflicts of the mind wear me down; slumber does not come easily as my swarming thoughts buzz like bees.

I push myself to fix the mistake. I push myself to make amends, trying to reverse the wrongdoing.

I claw at myself, dwelling on what has happened and tossing out accusations. Thrown into an ocean of doubt. Nothing works and I am left in the dust. The only thing I can do is learn from my past in order to grow, knowing not to make the same mistake again.

Grief

Grief pulls me underneath the hectic waves, the salty loch infecting my lungs. I thrash and kick, but I sink in devastation and despair. Grief fills me with fiery demons.

The waves dissolve and the madness fades. A serene flowing ripple of balance takes the place of the flooding and soon the sun is shining brightly again, replacing the cold, dark sea, turning it to a peaceful blue.

It is a cycling wheel of terror. There is the pulling of the hair and sobbing in the night, wishing so badly that they would come back from the dead and be in your presence. But they are not coming back, and a rotten sense of loneliness overcomes me.

What if I could have done something differently? What if I had said something sooner? What would have happened if one thing had gone differently?

Night becomes day. Soft weeping recalling cherished memories, acceptance of their passing. The cycle restarts, a tornado knocking me off my feet, a whirlwind of despair.

A destructive demon enters my body, tearing open my scorched flesh and gnawing at my conscience. When will the weeds of winter wither? When will the buds of a flower blossom once more? Planting seeds, day by day, hour by hour. I tend to my garden of hope, shining rays of light onto the darkened soil. The stones are cleared away. In place, grows a large angel oak.

When will the haunting nightmares of the dead fly away into the night? The maddening, inky blackness, the shadows which dance across the wall. They taunt me in the lonesome nightfall as skeleton hands scratch at my window, begging to be let inside. My father, his eyes are black holes in his face, staring into my frozen gaze in my dreams. His spirit, walking among my mind, breathing toxic chemicals into my lungs.

Dust gathers in the wind. The harsh breeze stings my skin, the world is blurry underneath the wrath of the storm. Shielding my eyes, I race towards shelter, watching fearfully as my world is overcome with an overwhelming tornado of grief.

Memories of the past and outlines of ghastly spirits roam in the dusty wind. They pop up unexpectedly like bills which weigh you down. Death is inevitable. Grief is inevitable. It pours hail stones into the atmosphere. It pours down a million emotions onto your shoulders. Will it ever vanish? Will the debilitating madness ever end?

The worst of the storm will pass. The heaviness of the waves will simmer to a rippling creek. Grief comes then goes. Wounds become patched and stitched. Over time, the death of people closest to you will seem like a distant memory, the pang of despair diminishing into simple sadness. Simple memories flood through my mind, flowing out like a waterfall slipping into a serene lake.

Beneath the cold, icy ground lies blossoms and daffodils. Dig deep, dig bravely and the gooey center of healing will show itself. The tree of hope will grow once more. Scarlet, flaxen and aqua blue colors will dance in my vision once more.

Grief is nothing but an obstacle. An obstacle which can be overcome. An obstacle which will pass.

A manifestation of celestial light rises above the gloomy skies. The beginning signs of spring bounce into sight.

My father, a shadow in the snowfall, fades with the dripping snowflakes. His footprints sealed into the soil. His soul consumed by the sun, melting the harsh season.

Grieving turns to sorrow. Sorrow turns to plain, passing thoughts. Then, slowly but surely, acceptance walks through the door, pushing the nauseating grief into a locked box and into the dusty darkness of the past.

In time, all wounds will heal.

Log Cabin of Memories

Darkness has made a nest in the house. There is an evil unseen locked within the bricks containing unspeakable horrors. A mere shadow of flames. I see somber reflections within the torn walls of old pain, of buried memories.

Stones cover the cursed soil, a poignant reminder of your lost, haunted soul. Lonesome screams resonate with singing crows. A fetid effluvia of corpses wafts through the air. A deathly etiolated figure roaming amid bones suffering an eternity of deafening silence.

There are bloody streaks across crackling walls. Echoes of panic-stricken shrieks. The house burns, my reflection stuck inside.

The decaying log cabin rots into ashes. The kitchen where you cooked pancakes has grown quiet; thorns and weeds tangle the walls and tear away the paint. The chairs made from oak collect dust as the dinner table no longer holds home-made meals.

The hooves of the horses have faded into the dust and faint neighs which once filled the paddocks can be heard in the stillness of the night. Their hooves overgrown, their manes entangled, and their once glossy coats are now dull with mats. Bugs crawl upon their flesh, latching themselves onto their bones.

Wild cats and hungry foxes make their way through the land, raiding what used to be a well-kept home. The cows have overrun the fences, their dead bodies lay upon the brown grass as scavengers feed upon their corpses.

Driving by, you would hardly recognize it as a once stunning ranch house filled with lively animals and kids climbing on trees, rolling through green grass. Expensive decorations used to cover the land, showing off the elegance of the log cabin house.

Murky water floats from the mossy pond and floods the ground. Metal wire has crumpled to the dirt, taken by dust and leaves.

The house which held our family now stands alone on the land with branches scratching at the windows. Rats run through the floors and gnaw at the wood. A pool of your blood stains the tiles. Your bones sink into the ground and the bedroom where you lay rots away, the scent of your cologne fades from the closet until the memory of you collapses.

Echoes of laughter are heard through the wooden walls; ghosts of children run through the bleak rooms. The large ranch house in which the little girl inside of me lived is now a ghost in the morbid blackness of the chilling night. Distant, haunting memories fade. The light from nostalgic moments slips away from the cabin until it is a forbidding silhouette in the gloom of nighttime.

Shadowy figures creep into the walls, invading the rooms and acting out illicit, dark activities. You let strangers in our house, and they sucked you into their twisted game, ruining you until you blew yourself away in the dreadful cabin full of sorrowful memories and tragic endings.

"Come home to me." You hauntingly whisper to me in the dark of night. You send memories of the cabin into my dreams, images of rotting horses and fire spreading throughout the barns and paddocks. You pull me towards that cabin, yearning for me to come and rescue you from the walls of that house.

I turn my head away. I ignore your words which drift into my head, yearning for me to come back and fall victim to the ghastly presence of my childhood home.

First Love

First love is delicate and pure. I am a newborn, bright-eyed dove soaring through cloudless skies with the wind blowing happily in my face. First love is bright colors and late-night talks. First love is swirling and heart-stopping passion. It covers me like a blanket and sends warmth from my head to my toes.

First love comes with first hugs, first kisses, first all-consuming emotions that lifts you high into the sky.

You took my hand and walked me down the road of blissful, red love. You held me close, showing me how love is supposed to feel. I relish your memory; you devoured me and ignited a beautiful light to burn within me. First love is dancing giddily and constant smiles. It is consistent conversations and nervous first dates. It is crashing into you like thunder and falling in your safe, strong arms.

I twiddle my thumbs and shuffle my feet around my first love. We glance at each other innocently. The expression on your face speaks loving words to my ears. We collapse in on each other in an affectionate embrace.

I discovered a red-hot ecstasy with you, your touch seeped into my skin and burned my bones. Your eyes beamed onto my face, brightening my vision, and causing the world to become vibrant. The love that I discovered with you was innocent and enchanting. Your rough, warm hand lay in mine, our fingers danced together, and you caressed my skin. The sensation of you being so close sent tingles throughout my skin and bones, excitement fluttered through my heart.

We were in the softness of the clouds; I felt safe and sound. But then the sky became dark and the storm knocked me off the clouds, I fell and sank into the ground, trying so desperately to reach you but my first love darted into the swirling darkness.

First love comes slowly then ends rapidly. First love comes with new beginnings and the discovery of each other. Will it last? Will it go on forever? I wish the fire would continue burning and the light never dim. I held onto you closely and maybe that was my inevitable downfall. Did I love too intensely? Was my desire for your presence too much to handle? Where did my first love go? How did it vanish so quickly?

You evaporated. My first love came to an end, the maddening loneliness took its place. Where did it go wrong? Your love cut me deep and eventually I bleed out at your feet. You wore a blank face and your heart became guarded. Shields covered your skin and your eyes were mere holes in your face.

First love is heavenly. First love brings you up then tears you down. You were my first love and my heart soars at the thought of the love you poured onto me. You were my first love, but it was not enough, and it became crushed into the ground. Smack. It is gone.

Lilacs

Aroma of lilacs
in a pitch-black room.
I recall our warmth
in the dusty solitude
our memories exhumed.

A dingy gloom
looming
in the
venomous
atmosphere.

I discover
an acoustic perfume
to drown out
the symphonies of silence
bringing doom
upon my abode.

Do Not Forget

Your memory of me is a glass on the edge, ready
to crash into pieces, swept into a dark bin where
no light can reach it. You push it away and resist
nostalgic memories which pull you apart, dissecting
you like an open frog on a metal table.

Dust gathers on the pages of our story. You stuff
the book into your closet, refusing to pick up
where you left off to begin a new chapter.

A trace of us is hidden within crumbling walls,
within cold sheets, within catastrophic memories.

Late night cuddling, your arms were strong, and your
cologne wafted throughout the room like delicious
freshly made bread and pastries in a bakery. Your eyes
shone with adoration and your head nuzzled my hair
tenderly like a dog tending to her newborn puppy.
Do not forget my jasmine perfume and the curves
of my body, do not forget my sweet, loving words
and the way my skin fit perfectly next to yours.

In the echoes of empty hours, your voice is an
insufferable bell roaring in my ear. We are apart yet
still connected in the silent cadaverous nightfall.

Cherished moments between us came then
passed. Yet, the memories remain.

Do not forget how you wished the nights of passionate
embracing could last forever. I was your queen and
you were my king, we sat high on thrones and coated
each other with gifts and flowers. You swept in on your
red carriage and drove us into a blissful land where
only the two of us existed in our closed in bubble.

Do you think of me while you fall asleep in your
nest where I lie? My bare skin touching yours. We
were an entanglement of legs and arms, reaching
for each other in the quiet, coldness of the night.

"I need some time away."

You spoke haunting words. There is a yearning within
me to beg you to wait for me while I struggle to make
peace with my demons. I beg you to promise that
you will cheer me on silently and not give up.

Do not forget me.
For I shall never forget you and your
tempting, adoring memory
which is becoming too far away.

Betrayal

You cut me open and left me to bleed; my blood spilled onto the floor and stained your skin with red. The promises you spoke wilted into sour lies which spilled from your tongue, engulfing me with a fiery sadness. Your comforting hands and tender lips fell away and, in their place, came your sharp nails, cold eyes and teeth which bare daggers.

The elixir of love has exited your system.

How did nights of passion and fondness in your heart come to sleepless nights of tossing and turning with tear stained eyes? My bed remains empty; the sheets are made of ice. My flesh is frozen and cold like the wintry breeze. The rooms are dark; shadows dance on the walls, taunting me, reminding me of the newfound loneliness which roam these halls.

Your betrayal stings my skin and buries me into the dirt. A volcano of lava burns within me from the inside out, crackling in my bones. I collapse into the wreckage of your disappearance and haunting, lost words.

What did I do wrong? Why would you lie and leave me like that? Had any of your endearing words been true? Why would you betray me like that?

I had merely been an innocent girl flitting through life searching for someone to cherish me and not fly away. You caught me off guard and destroyed that innocence, leaving me crushed and smeared on the ground.

Why would you bother catching me in your rough hands? You took me in then tossed me away. Your tongue is sinful, your heart is rotten. You play the victim and place the blame onto me when you are the true villain. I am merely your toy to play with. You toss the promise of the one thing you would not do.

Jealousy

I gallop towards you, my heart aching
for your soothing touch.

Too late, too slow.

Your burning gaze rests upon the beauty of the new
angel. I am a fading skeleton in your mind. My devotion
towards you breaks my limbs. I am lying on the ground,
broken and helpless as you bury yourself in her presence.

Was I not enough for your greedy hands?
You took your fill then tossed me. I became
stranded in quicksand. I sink into my devotion
towards you which becomes my downfall.

There is a powerful fire blazing within my burning
soul. You shut my pain out and speak kind words to
the angel who glowingly shines in your world. Blame
is placed upon my shoulders; you escape the trial
and stand freely as I am consumed with bitterness.

Sweet hellos echo from your lips, you smile towards
everybody but me who sparkles brighter than the sun.
Your teeth gleam while you bare them, your lips turned
upward. I am a mere bystander watching you run away
into the horizon, disappearing from my squinted vision.

I no longer flourish under your gaze. Your eyes shift away, and I sink into darkness. You dance around the angel like a prancing deer. There is a gnawing, red hot envy which burns my skin until it is melting off my bones into your hands which no longer bear the warmth of love. You take your cold hand and throw daggers into my skin, my body a decaying building which you can corrupt.

You admire her splendor and I stand in the shadows, my glamor no longer stunning to your gaze. A resentment fills me from head to toe; you flit away to a new lover and I sorrowfully watch, powerless to intervene, as the light of my life is gone from my sight without even a goodbye.

Consider me gone, you have moved on to a fresh start. Consider me gone. I float into the wind, gone from your burning presence. I realize I am no longer needed in your bleak eyes.

Too Close

Too close, I think while I scoot further away on
the cushioned seat. Your hands are tight on the
wheel, your head turned away. The wheels squeak
rapidly on the paved road. The music turned
up high, the deafening silence in the air

Too close, I think while my heart beats quick. Too close, I
think to myself while I lean my head against the window.

Too close to you, too close to the memories that seem to be
slipping from my grip. Too close, the words fly through
me as I resist the urge to hold your rough, warm hand.

You are too close. My control is fading. I yearn for your
body to be close to mine. My defense crumbles to dust. My
pleading eyes drift towards you. There is so much to say
but the words are frozen in my mouth. I chew on them,
they threaten to spill out, but they never do. Suddenly the
closeness is evaporating and being blown out the window.

Your seat is inches from mine but the distance
between us is like the sun and the moon

We dance around each other like two timid
children. We avoid eye contact, fearing the
memories in our reflection. Too close, we run in
opposite directions, leaving our hearts behind.

Too close and not close enough. We are too close
and I back away into the shadows. Cowering
away from your presence. Too close.

Let Me In

You entangle yourself
in a thick cloth
it wraps around you
like a swarm of moths.

Fire shoots from my hands
onto your shield
but it melts away.

I slip on your blanket of ice
my bones cracking
blood staining my heart.

You wash away the stains
of the wreckage.

Show Me Your Heart

All I wish is to see dark red carnations
blooming from your hands.

Show me your heart, pour your tears out and rip your
thick skin open for me to peer into. Let your eyes bleed
emotion, let your heart be open for me! You are sly like
a snake as you swim around me. Oh, please let the frost
of your coldness thaw out to warm, trickling honey.

Show me your scarlet colors and joyful greetings. Let
me reach inside you to pull out the light and hang
it above our heads like mistletoe. You stand with
your broad back facing me, there is a tall, brick wall
built around you, daggers and shields are hung atop,
acting as your guard. Show me your heart! Show
me your love! Show me your blissful warmth! You
are a robot as you cunningly move past me, your
gaze straight ahead and your feet pacing quickly.

Oh, won't you cry for me? Show me your sentiments
and let them rain down on me like drizzling rain. What
must I do to see if you are feeling the same pain as I?
Show me something, show me your sweet, delicate
compassion! Why must you act so insensitive?

I wait with agony growing in my heart for you to turn the key and open yourself to me. You are a closed door with your lock latched tightly and your heart clotted with bleakness.

I explore the depths of your soul. I abhor the way you ignore my desperate pleas. I will do more to express that I adore you forevermore. I bury our memories underneath a sycamore tree. I speak a promise to restore your amour fou towards me.

You turn away from me, standing in the sun, leaving me in the night of the day. I keep on loving you, eternally wondering when I will see your heart once more.

 *IV*

Elegance of the Horse

The saddle is placed underneath my thighs which squeeze the sides of the pacing beast. The wind blows through my mane, my hands grip the leather connected to the head. The hooves pound against the dirt, the nose of the beast flaring, its eyes blazing wildly as we soar together and become one.

There is an elegance in the way the horse holds herself, she dances and twirls in the sun, galloping across the meadow, floating like a beautiful flower. She sings in the night and holds herself high. My pale hand glides across her fur. My nose gobbles up the scent of hay. Her breath fans my face, covered in sweat. Her mouth licks my hand filled with gifts.

A smile grows upon my delicate face as I sit upon her trusting throne. She carries me protectively. We discovered the world together, trailing through the land and staking claim over the soil in which she walks over. Her coat glistens in the sun as she laps at water which falls like rain from the rocks. She is a deer as she prances across the grass, her tail held high, her head holding a force of elegance.

She is beauty in the day, she is glamour in the night. She is as free as the birds and as strong as a bull. She shines like the sun, her white coat as pure as a dove. I walk her to the edge and let her go, she trots out of sight, free to wander gracefully on her own as she glides through the breeze.

Her exquisiteness is stunning; she is delicate like a rose I hold to my heart and squeeze tight, taking in her wild smell and letting it sweep me away into blissful places. The elegance of the horse is breathtaking, and I become captivated by her large, gentle body which I ride as she takes me away into an opulent paradise.

Luxury

She is mystery in the day
and eloquent glamor in the night.

She sails on the stars,
bathing in her elegance.

Happiness

Where do you find happiness? they inquisitively ask,
oblivious to the secrets of the universe that are coated
all around. Happiness dances around, teetering on
the edge of the cliff, slipping away so easily. They
catch it in their hands like fireflies, the light shining
in their wondrous eyes. They release it into the
air. It flies into the sky, too far to run towards.

Happiness is warm nights with your lover, lying by the
burning fire while you passionately entangle your limbs
with each other. Happiness is quiet bike rides in the
morning when the dew is still fresh on the mowed grass. It
is listening to the birds chirping songs in the early dawn.

Happiness is discovered within pouring bright colors on a
canvas and creating a masterpiece from your own hands.
Happiness is tending to your delicate needs, cradling your
soul, and becoming one with yourself. You find happiness
in the little things that flutter by in the day. The greetings
that drip from strangers' lips, the polite hand that holds
the door open, the friendly smiles on the faces of peers.

It is walking through a garden and humming
peacefully while your fingers trail along the
petals of red, pink, and purple flowers, admiring
the flowers that bloom in the grass.

There is pleasure in holding your dog and inhaling their fur in your nose, taking in their musky scent. There is exhilaration in soaring through a paved trail, your feet leaving behind dust as they take you to a peaceful destination. There's pleasure in sitting by the pond and swishing your feet in the swaying, calm water as you listen to the sounds of the waves tumbling through the air.

Happiness is found within yourself once you accept and love the ugly along with the beauty. Happiness comes in tides; you are pulled into the flow of the bliss and it consumes you. Just like the moon, it pulls you out and you are thrown into a surging current of unease. Happiness is not handed to you like candy, it is developed and created within your own hands. Happiness is the joy you find in everyday life, it flows with the wind and flies around your face, taunting you with its promises of bliss.

I will tell you; I say to them confidently. My heart beats, a tingly delight surging within me. Happiness does not exist; it is a word designed to distract you from the truth. Eternal happiness is a myth which hangs above heads and dances in the shadows. What matters is the cheery, gratifying moments in life which lift you up and sings songs of elation.

Happiness does not ruffle its wings, preparing to soar into the sunset. Happiness comes out to play only when you know where to look to uncover it. It does not leave like a father who abandons his innocent children, happiness is always right there beside you, holding your hand, waiting for you to climb out of the darkness to acknowledge the light and fall into it, coating yourself with pure delight.

Healing

My body grows fresh bones.

The whirling pitch black storm that fumes and builds
within me burns horrendously. It melts my flesh and
tears at my eyes, stabbing holes in my face. Pain radiates
through my rattling bones. I am crushed into the dirt as
peers dance over my helpless, sagging corpse. The demons
whisper words as bitter as unsweetened chocolate.

There is a light at the end of the infinite, inky tunnel.
Exhaustion pushes me as I collapse into the quicksand.
Faint voices whisper my name in the dark vastness
of a suffocating scorching volcano. Ancient souls
save me from the paralyzing ashy nuclear winter.
A single strand of golden stars twinkles within the
barren cosmic boneyard containing fallen dreams.

My weak limbs carry me towards the unknown edge
of the pit, the sun glows as it appears on the edge of
vision. The darkness dims, a red phoenix lifts me into the
sunset, the dusk turns into day as the murky shadows
of the past floats into the sky, releasing me of the chains
that were secured around my ankles and throat.

When you cannot breathe, when the waves swallow
you, when panic rises, when the mournful winter buries
you, breathe deep. Inhale the rosy scent of blossoming
gardens. Remove the black veil, bathing in sunlight.

I step into the boat of wonder as it floats down the tranquil stream of blue. Colorful koi fish swim alongside as they skip through the rippling current. The future is bright. I peer ahead into the light, a rainbow gleams in the warming sunlight. A garden is planted onto my skin, roses and dandelions weaving around me.

My mind is cleared. The abyss is covered with soil and a meadow grows in its place. I frolic through a majestic meadow, the scent of jasmine wafting through my nostrils. I walk out of hell. Dawn rises, I smile.

The memory of abuse is far away. The memory of a chaotic childhood is fading. The memory of my father is no longer a silent killer. The stabbing pain no longer controls me. I sit in the front seat and drive down the path of forgiveness and sunshine.

When in doubt, I remind myself of the things that I love. I remind myself to inhale fresh air when I am drowning in a storm of turmoil.

I Am Ready

The past is washed away into the ocean. Time passes by rapidly. You are a new man, your hair tumbling down your forehead. You sail through your life at ease, the darkness drifts away and you are pulled back from the edge of the daunting cliff. I am a new woman, my skin fresh and my hair thick, a merry bounce is seen in my step as I float among the clouds. There is a yearning for your arms to swarm around my body as you engulf me like the sun on a bright day.

I am ready, I say while I twirl around you like a swan. I am ready, I whisper. My eyes flutter and my heart leaps.

There's readiness in my eyes. The darkness ebbs away into the atmosphere. There is a well-lit luminosity looming above my head. I swim through the delicate stars, yearning for your company in the igniting radiance of the world. Your striking handsomeness burns bright in my eyes. I become lost in your beaming eyes as warm as the golden sun. Your smile is breathtaking in my vision. You flash your pearly, white teeth towards me adoringly.

We both made mistakes, but they become ash as the bitterness of the past fades away. A sweet, newfound love makes its way into the open, creating room for new memories to be made from the dust, rising into the air like a flaming, passionate fire.

I am ready, I say while we entwine our fingers and walk among the flowers together. We sink into the illuminating sunset with each other. We listen to an ocean's song. We float into an enchanting fairyland, frolicking through starlight meadows. We start over with fresh minds and open hearts.

No Words Needed

Your lips are silent. Your mouth is sewn shut. I hear your gentle words through your tender eyes and sweet, colorful smile. Your hands speak of love. Your caresses tell me of a passionate fire burning in your chest at the sight of my radiating presence as they glide down my tingling skin. My eyes dart over to yours and my lips turn upward as your eyes meet mine in the middle. You gaze at me as if I am a princess dressed in a lovely dress and red high heels. There are no words needed as your body tells me what you are thinking. The softness of your steps, the gleeful shine in your eyes, your head which nuzzles mine.

I hesitantly reach my hand over to yours and our fingers touch; sparks fly upwards from our skin and erupt into fireworks in the sky. Your hands squeeze mine, sending butterflies into my heart.

My eyes close with contentment and
my body sinks into yours.
There is no need to say I love you; I can feel it
in the warmth of your skin and the fondness of
your touch as you pull me close with an intention
of never letting me go as we fall into bliss.

The Memory of Christmas

The season of merriment comes upon me. I sit in my apartment. The only company I have is Violet. She breathes soundly in the twinkling of the night. There are soft melodies drifting through the walls, speaking of snow, reindeer, and bells. There is a smile placed upon my face as I sip hot cocoa and sink into a velvety quilt, covering my shivering body.

Decorations hang upon the walls and sit on top of the white counters, reminding me of Christmas as a child.

I can see my siblings sitting around the large Christmas tree in the middle of the floor which gives off a strong smell of figs, their eyes are hopeful and curious as they stare at the wrapped boxes as if they were wondrous secrets. My father captures moments with his Nikon camera as my mother smiles upon her children.

The memory of Christmas is faded in my mind. I vaguely recall holidays with family as we celebrated the joy of the season. Scents of baked cookies and frosted cupcakes flood into my senses, fresh meals, and warm milk seep down my throat into my grumbling stomach.

Fuzzy socks cover my chilled feet; there is a wintry breeze in the atmosphere as a white blanket covers the land outside my foggy window. Echoes of laughter wade through the air as children slide down the harrowing, icy land. Parents clap their hands and their cheery voices follow the children as they play.

I peer outside, seeing my siblings and I tossing balls of snow at each other. My dog in the distance licking at the snow, laughter and screaming drifting throughout the breezy air. Bells ring in my ears as reindeer fly over the roof, their majestic bodies sliding gracefully through the night.

"Merry Christmas," I whisper to myself in the silence and solitude of the nighttime. The stars shimmer among the grey clouds, the snow resembling ash in the dark.

The memory of Christmas sinks. I replace those chaotic memories of the season with new, joyous moments of the present. The little girl inside of me embraces me. I give her the Christmas she constantly yearned for, filled with peace and festive times without any signs of anguish.

Walking Amid the Gravestones

My feet crunch on leaves, they carry me into the eerie cemetery. Ghosts tap my shoulders and whisper sorrowful moans in my ears. My fingers trace gravestones while I walk past them. Chills pass through my skin. I become aware of the dead bodies which lie beneath my feet.

Your name comes up on the stone. I collapse into the ground. I stare at the spot where you lie. My hand touches the cold stone, tracing the faded words. A breeze flows through my hair and the sun shines down onto me, despite the bitter gelidity which seeps into my heart. Tears pour down my cheeks as the memory of you crashes into me like a train.

Your fatherly smile, the joy on your face when you would catch sight of your daughters. Your adoring words and the confidence in your stride. I push away the nagging thoughts of your destruction. You took your demons to the grave, but I release them from your grip while forgiveness washes over me.

"It's okay, you can rest now," I tell you softly. You fall into a peaceful slumber in your death as the weight lifts from your spirit. I ponder over what life might have been like if you never fell victim to the world of drugs and darkness.

You are gone. The thoughts are merely empty dreams. I rise from the ground as a sense of serenity flows among me. You are gone and everything is going to be okay. You are gone, and I cannot control what happened.

I turn my back and continue walking amid the endless gravestones, your memory fresh and soft in my mind. Your wrongdoings are no longer holding me down. The weights of sadness replaced with nostalgic gratitude for the time spent with you when you still walked among the living.

Now you lie among the gravestones in the dead of night. You sink into a peaceful slumber in paradise. Light consumes your once troubled spirit, your sins washed away into the sea, ridding you of the rotten apple that filled your core. You reach out your hand and I take it into mine. We walk together, the ugly foulness that stood between us no longer present as it is swept away by a daughterly love for her father.

I am free, I think to myself joyously as I have finally let go of the consuming darkness and grief. I stroll into a new chapter of my bright, optimistic life. I release myself from the cage I had been trapped inside of. No longer controlled by the itching worry or desperation for a distraction from my stabbing pain.

I walk amid the gravestones, finding the exit to the road and walking among the paved concrete as I leave behind my sorrow. *I am free*, I think while I soar like a dove to a dazzling, fresh beginning.

His Touch

"Touch me," I whisper into the quiet softness of nightfall.
Shimmering stars fall upon my skin while he lays
his fingers across me. Red, blissful fire consumes
my bones as he rattles me to the core.
His touch soothes my cloudy worries and brings
peace upon the land of my body. I am his canvas.
His touch paints my skin pink. He frees me of
the vines entangling my flesh, planting rosy
apples and sunflowers upon my white shell.

Twilight Beauty

I dance in the twilight, glowing like a comet passing
through the shining dark. I sing in the silence of the
night, serenading my lover with passionate, swirling
notes of love. I twirl with the wind in my crimson sun
dress. I swim with the swans in the river of tranquility.

I have red ribbons woven into my hair and
pink lipstick glazed across my cherry lips.

"Come with me to the land of paradise," I tell my
sweet lover. I flutter away like a butterfly.
He follows me like a magnet, entranced by my
flaming, exquisite beauty. The paleness of my
skin shines in the twilight evening. Petals cover
the pavement; doves soar beneath the moon.
His voice is a lullaby in my ears as tender words escape
your instrument. We dance together in the twilight,
watching the city lights burn. We take claim of the night.

I dare you to enter my darkling world. I beg you
to take a breath dive into my sea of inky shape and
shadow. Transform the woods of terror into an
enchanted forest filled with refreshing waterfalls.

Nothing to Hide

I am filled with lies and secrets.

When it comes to you
my affection is no secret.

My blazing red passion
is the one truth
in my deceitful life.

Desolate nights
bears a nebulous darkness.

I am a fish
drowning on dry land.
I am a skeleton
decaying underneath piles
of suffocating soil

Tonight
with you
there is an aroma of roses
underneath the crystalline moonlight
there is a murmur
of your mellifluous voice.

You are an angel
in my world
filled with wicked demons.

Wake Up to You

Morning arrives, my heart falls into an abyss, eyes filled with disdain. I wish I could wake up to your sweet face when the sun rises. I wish I could wake up to your strong arms embracing my body in the early dawn. The sheets beneath me become unfriendly. They squeal mockingly with their emptiness. The open space in my bed is a mere reminder of your disappearance. Just once more I wish I could lie in your loving embrace.

Your pillow has been long gone and your warmth left months ago. All I am left with are empty wishes and cold skin. I lie in the pouring rain and breezy wind. Can you feel me when you lie in bed? Can you hear me when I call for you in the night? Can you remember the feel of my skin when you open your eyes in the dawn of morning?

We become a lost dream.

We become strangers in the night.

Do Not Give Up

Bear with me, I tell you with desperation in my gaze.
You hold me tight in the twilight night, whispering
words of tenderness. You sing lullabies of hope.

My heart longs for your patience, your distance
pestering me. I solemnly spoke of fondness for your
soul, hoping that is enough for you to stay.

You are like the dandelions rising in the beginnings
of the unclouded season of spring, bringing spurts
of giddiness and long walks in the garden.

Darkness swept over the beauty of the soil.
Trees lost their leaves and my skin turned cold
from the virulent nights. White blankets of frost
covered your heart. My love was not enough.

Maybe one day, when we are balanced like yin
and yang, our red passion can begin anew.

You came in like gentle, crashing waves and
flooded me with a glowing radiance.

I find my way back to wanting you. But if you do
not find your way back to me, I will know it is time
to pack my bags and journey to another home.

I will bloom again when the winter passes, when the
ice thaws out, when my garden grows once more.

Somebody You Long For

I wish I could be somebody you long for in the nightfall when your mind is quiet. I wish to be somebody you think of while you are going about your day. I wish to be somebody you pull out the ring for while you are on your knees. I wish to be somebody you come home to at the end of the day, your smile wide as you focus your gaze on me.

If only you craved my presence like I ache for your heart.

Crash into You

You are a soft cloud. I fall through the air, crashing
into your warmth. You shield me from the edges
of basalt stones which threaten to pierce my skin.
I crash into you with the force of lightning. You
catch me, then whisper you will never let me go.

You crashed into me like a thousand falling
stars, blowing my sorrow away and creating a
sun which burns beautifully inside of me.

Your eyes contain rays of warm golden sunshine. We
dive into a passionate scarlet tide. We travel to a place so
lovely made of rosy pearls and mystic waters My gardens
flourish and the stars shine if you are here by my side

Fate

"You can't fight fate,"
I say while you tug away.
Your faith slipping, your passion withering.

"You can't fight fate,"
I say while you fly towards me once more,
engulfing me with your tender wings.

Everything that is
meant to be
will always come back.

The universe
is always
listening.

My King

There is tenderness in his touch when
he paints my skin with tulips.
There is softness in his delicate breath
when he lights the way in the fog.

There is a crown upon his head.
He is my king; I am his queen. Together we
storm the castle of passion and make our home
inside each other's hearts. We gaze upon magical
sunsets encompassed by enchanted meadows.
Soft feathered sapphire birds sing melodic lullabies,
your lips planting crimson kisses
upon my incandescent flesh.

You are there, amid tumultuous storms. You are there,
amid deafening darkness. I am rescued by a vision of
you. You take my hand, leading me towards the radiating
light. You are a beacon of hope in a world filled with tar.

Together, we thrive.

Fatherly Warmth

A warm day wrapped with heavenly sensations,
you held yourself highly.
The motorcycle had been our carriage,
we were carried by the wind.

Tattoos upon his skin
glistened in the sun.
His curly black hair shielded my vision.
The world passed by in a blur.

In that moment,
he was my father,
I was his daughter.
.

For a moment, you transformed into a mighty god.
For a moment, I was no longer your
doll covered with weeds.
We were one as we soared like free
birds, your demons at bay.

Winter Land

The land outside contains a tranquil silence in
the empty dusk. A white blanket of ice
creates an endless pool among the soil.
The sky turns to an illuminating wintry gloom.
The sun perishes into falling stars.
A lone doe frolics gracefully among
the sheets, hiding within
the barren trees. The moonlight of the sky ignites a
brightness to show her the path towards her herd as
she wanders through the bitterness of the night.

Songs of Sorrow

The wind blows
across this land.

The lonesome sparrow
flows through
the blustery mournful woods
in the breeze of the storm
screaming echoes of loss.

Warm Colors

Lead me into the warm colors of bliss. Paint my lips
red. Cover my heart with exploding butterflies while
you paint swirling, eloquent pigments on my skin.

My heart blooms in your glamorous presence.
Our souls are the same pieces of soaring stars.
You are my inspiration for beauty and poetic tunes. You
release drizzling rainbows when my clouds are grey
when there was merely pain. You planted seeds into my
flesh which rise into sunflowers. I bathe in your breath,
becoming refreshed. There are no regrets in loving you.

Quiet

Silence accompanies the cities in the moonlit nightfall.
The animals frolicking in the darkness
are camouflaged from harm
while they settle down
in their nests of comfort.

The man listens to the rainfall
while he drives home to his kids,
their little faces
pressed against the window.

A lone car roaming
in the emptiness of the evening,
soft tunes playing in the dark.

Candles burn in the frames
of warm homes and cooked dinners
the neighborhood becomes still in the dusk.

A mourning widow sitting by her bed,
staring at the frame
she silently weeps for her lost lover.

He whispers in her ear,
"I'm still here."

The night becomes deathly quiet.
There is beauty in the hush
while souls are laid to rest,
welcoming the peaceful quiet
in the hours of darkness.

Silent Solitude

Empty, squeaky escalator,
pacing up and down.

Skeletons taunting
my heart.

Ghosts of families
float around.

A crushing silence.

A shadow
my father
sits beside me
holding my hand.

"You're not alone,"

A chilling whisper.

He disappears
into the dusk.

I listen to planes flying by.

Tranquil Waters

I could dive
into the baby blue ocean
with you.

We discover
the beauty
of each other.

We float
into the sunset
filled with pink
and violet pigments.

There is something gentle
in the way
you gaze at me.

I could swim
in your sweet touch
for eternity.

Backbone

I could have made it
on my own
but with your love
my strength doubled.

You felt like home.
I soared like an eagle.

Good for Me

Winter hugs my flesh.

Crackling hints of solitude
seep out of holes
in my desolate heart.

The wings of a king
embrace my decaying skin.

Icy, prickling thorns
wither away.

Golden rays of light
paint my skin.

Your grace
is carved
into my lungs.

I have found
my home
in your warmth.

Mindfulness

The night forest; a magical haven. Cowering in the dark, camouflaged within bark. Drifting in time to a lighter era of love and peace. Stuck within my whirling mind. I live within a fantasy; I inhale potions of inevitable madness.

The curtains open, everybody has left.

Where did I go wrong?

Consumed with delusions,

hanging onto old grudges.

Hanging onto the past.

Let go.

Let go.

I plead and scream at myself.

I close my eyes. I open my chakras
and release rotting memories.

In the moment, I do not let my mind
wander. I do not let myself overthink.

I teach myself to flow with the current. I surrender,
I put my faith into the universe. I soar alongside
doves, enjoying the present moment.

The future is a question, it cannot be known. The past has come and gone, nothing more I can do. All I can do, is be mindful and let go of the mind numbing voices of guilt and sorrow.

Forgiveness

It is not easy to forgive my destroyers. It is not easy
to cut open my flesh and let my blood spill around
their feet. It is not easy to open the cage and to let my
heart fly. Wicked words and harmful poison haunt my
fragile psyche. An iceberg of damage, a world of pain.
It is not easy to forget when the wounds cut deep.

If it means finding eternal welfare and being
freed of these memories, I will search for
forgiveness. If it means discovering sacred healing,
then I will journey towards soft clouds.

If I cannot forgive, then I will never forget. If
I cannot forgive, then I will forever be frozen,
tumbling through dark, wintry storms.

The secret to moving on is acceptance and self-awareness.
For years, resentment filled my dead heart. In time, the ice
thawed, and my vision contains colors and butterflies.

Serenity has made its way into my soul.

Self-Love

I bury myself underneath a world of blame. My vision
catches sight of abandonment, it must be my fault.
Am I never good enough? The core of my soul weeps
and shivers, the memory of loved ones walking away
claws at me. I need them. I cannot survive without
their love, without their attention. My hands shake,
I watch them coddle other souls. I watch them talk
sweetly to everybody except me. Perhaps this is a
punishment. Perhaps I did something wrong.

Sinking underneath tar and quicksand, blending
with shadows, and holding hands with demons.

I am peering through glass. Voices echoing a
stony solitude. I am pounding and banging. Can
anyone hear me? Drowning within a night sea.
Stars fading, bleak faces staring through me.

fading

fading

They are too far to reach. My plea

to be seen

to be heard

is lost within the booming wind.

Crumbling into ash. I stitch myself back together.

I do not need them. I paint a canvas of beauty upon myself. My heart grows within my bones. When I weep in the darkness, I pat my own back and tell myself it will be alright. To be better and to love myself, I learned I must hit rock bottom to find the light again.

Vile guilt no longer follows me into my nightmarish dreams. The glass breaks, I sweep away the wreckage and tend to my own needs.

To truly forgive myself, to truly accept myself for the good and the ugly, I must love myself. I must reach down into my gut and wipe the cobwebs away.

Without self-love, happiness is hard to reach. I am worth it, I am enough.

I do not need approval, because I know I am doing well.

Bloom

I stand tall and mighty like a splendid oak tree.

There is growth in my bones,
smiles placed upon my face.
The beat of my heart
pumps at a delightful pace.

There is a serene silence in the air.

I plant seeds of hope
within my mystical fairyland.

My garden of beauty blossoms.

I rise like a newborn phoenix
from the darkened soil
soaring into the sun
shining like a twinkling star.

There is a manifestation
of an ephemeral light
in the beginning signs
of spring.

I sail on a sea of lullabies.
I wave goodbye
to the bruises
which paralyze my bones.

I am a rising bud
of an earthy redolent flower
blooming brilliantly.

I am a survivor
of a bone breaking,
suffocating avalanche.

I am a survivor
in the midst
of murderous pain.

CPSIA information can be obtained
at www.ICGtesting.com
Printed in the USA
BVHW040949270720
584745BV00013B/999